SCHOOL AND COMMUNITY IN THE THIRD WORLD

School and Community in the Third World

M.E. SINCLAIR
WITH KEVIN LILLIS

CROOM HELM LONDON

in association with

THE INSTITUTE OF DEVELOPMENT STUDIES, SUSSEX

Croom Helm Ltd, 2-10 St John's Road, London SW11

British Library Cataloguing in Publication Data

Sinclair, M E
School and community in the third world.
1. Community development
2. Underdeveloped areas – Education
3. Community schools
I. Title
370.19'4'091724 HN49.C6

ISBN 0-7099-0323-5

Printed and bound in Great Britain by
Redwood Burn Limited
Trowbridge & Esher

CONTENTS

ACKNOWLEDGEMENTS

The study of which this book is the chief product was financed by a grant from the Ministry of Overseas Development in London and based in the Institute of Development Studies at the University of Sussex.

Thanks are especially due to Mr W.A. Dodd, Chief Education Adviser at the Ministry of Overseas Development, Professors Ronald Dore and Richard Jolly at the Institute and Mr Desmond Hogan of the Education Area of the University for their help, encouragement and suggestions. In particular, Dr John Oxenham of the Institute was responsible for launching the study and shared in the overall process of its development.

The field experience, which made interpreting the literature of 'relevant' education much easier, was owed to the Ford Foundation: it financed a first hand study of schooling related to work in India and Sri Lanka.

Numerous educators in Sri Lanka and India have afforded kindness, consideration and time to one who was variously colleague, up-country researcher and visitor. Without their endless tolerance and courtesy, this venture would have been immeasurably poorer. Our gratitude to them is great.

M.E. Sinclair
Kevin Lillis

Falmer, Sussex

SCHOOL AND COMMUNITY IN THE THIRD WORLD

INTRODUCTION

T.R. Batten (1959) in his review of attempts to use the school as a vehicle for community development emphasised the limitations of what the teacher could do with one pair of hands, modest training and an often unreceptive 'client' community. The flow of projects designed to relate the work of the school more closely to the life and work of the local community has continued unabated, however, as governments of Third World countries in every continent have felt the need for more relevant schooling.

There has been a major shift of emphasis since Batten's review. On the one hand there has been a substantial effort in most Third World countries to establish specialised agencies and extension services designed to introduce modern agricultural practices, assist in the development of cottage industries and raise health standards in an overall strategy of rural development. The temptation to think of the school as a major, or even sole, vehicle for undertaking this kind of community development programme has, therefore, declined. On the other hand, the vast expansion in school enrolments has generated a new, or much aggravated, problem – the dissatisfaction of qualified school-leavers who are unable to gain access to the modern sector employment they desire. A persistent belief is that schools, by introducing more relevant programmes, can overcome young people's frustrations and ensure their willingness to participate in the life and work of their home communities. The differential in earnings between persons in modern sector employment and persons in the traditional sector sets a limit, however, to the school's potential to achieve this.

The desires to ameliorate school-leaver frustration, and in some instances to use the school directly as an agency for the promotion of rural uplift, have, nevertheless, led to many contemporary experiments in Third World countries; and the issue is a very live one in these countries and in international agencies such as UNESCO.

There are, though, no simple answers. While one meets enthusiasts who have direct personal experience of a successful venture, one also meets persons with a historical bent who suggest that past experience proves conclusively the inevitability of failure. One meets also persons depressed by practical experience of the difficulties experienced in launching this type of programme and such encounters may point, if not towards failure, at least towards returns disproportionately small in relation to the effort expended.

Looked at in academic terms, the question of whether schools should be directly involved with the world of work and community uplift is very open, especially in view of a dominant belief that schools are units of socialisation, agents of literacy and numeracy and, most importantly, agents of upward social mobility. The present study is concerned not so much to provide conclusive answers as to bring together in a systematic way some evidence from past and contemporary experience. Because of the political nature of decisions relating to these diversified programmes they have wide social implications and the matter will not rest on academic judgement. Politicians may decide in favour of a work experience or community-oriented programme, leaving educators to decide upon the process of implementation. A second issue to be considered is, therefore, the relative merit of different approaches to making work experience and other activities an integral part of schooling. Are there certain paths to failure? (Yes!) Are there certain paths to success? (No!) Accordingly, this study attempts simply to identify some guidelines for developing programmes in a way which will best overcome the numerous constraints imposed by lack of material resources, lack of teachers with training in the necessary skills, and parental concern with examination results.

It is necessary to make two points of definition. Since 'primary' education has been variously interpreted as ranging from four to eight years of schooling, an alternative limitation of scope was to use the concept of the 'open-access' period of education or the 'basic cycle' (the period of education which is effectively open without restriction to children of modest means in a not too remote area – the effective period of 'mass education' at a given point in time). By definition this is the phase of education from which large numbers of children graduate. In any given country the duration of 'open access' or basic schooling defined in this way will increase over time as the number of schools at higher levels is expanded. It may progress from four years to six or eight.

The analysis focuses mainly upon six past 'relevance' innovations, i.e. Mexico's Rural Schools, Turkey's Village Institutes, Gandhian Basic Education, the Philippines Community Schools, the 1950s Tanganyika Agricultural Programme, Rural Education Centres in Upper Volta. Illustrations are, however, taken from more contemporary initiatives, e.g. education for self-reliance in Tanzania; pre-vocational studies in Sri Lanka; the basic secondary innovations in Cuba. After discussion of the development of the six case-studies in Part One of this book, the limitations of the strategies utilised are analysed in Part Two. Part Three discusses the overall processes of the management of these innovations utilising the analytical model developed by Bolam (1975) of change-agents in System innovation.

A second point of definition. The term 'relevant' in the project title could have opened the study to a consideration of the total process of educational change in the Third World, replacing a 'Western' curriculum by topics of study drawn from national history and culture and the local environment. From necessity, however, it has been taken more narrowly to comprise educational relevant to the development of local institutions, to health, nutrition and similar themes as well as the world of productive work, of agriculture and crafts. Especial attention has been paid to the latter topic, namely to work-related programmes in the schools, since this has been the focus of a number of recent initiatives. This review gives priority to ventures which incorporate practical activities, either alone or in conjunction with theoretical studies. Some mention is also made (notably in the opening and closing chapters) of the further option of developing 'environmental studies' and similar programmes.

One point of terminology may be mentioned here. For the sake of brevity, the programmes under discussion are frequently referred to by the simple title of 'relevance' programmes. This seemed preferable to a repeated listing of programme components or the clumsy phrase 'work experience and community-related programmes'.

Part One
RELEVANT EDUCATION

1 RELEVANT EDUCATION – A RECURRING THEME

The call for more relevant educational programmes was a marked feature of the educational scene towards the end of the 1960s. Militant students the world over proclaimed that their curricula excluded vital social issues. The sociologists of education pointed out that the language and content of schooling related to the lifestyles of the middle classes and lacked relevance to the experience of the working-class child. Educational planners noted that the qualitative aspects of educational planning had been neglected, suggesting that the expansion of schooling in Third World countries should be accompanied by curricular changes that would make it more relevant to the life and work of their mainly rural communities.[1] Innovative educators throughout the world have continued in the 1970s to work towards the ideal of more relevant and diversified schooling, even though 'relevance' as a catch-phrase or slogan has faded from the headlines. Ideas such as the building of school-community links and links of various kinds with the world of employment are under exploration in both industrialised and Third World countries together with attempts to introduce relevance through new curricula in fields such as social, environmental or integrated studies.

The search for relevance has a long history – indeed, the initiation of mass schooling in almost every country has led to a debate on this topic. The conservative elements in nineteenth-century England believed that the servant class should have no more schooling than was required for them to read the Bible: writing and arithmetic were not relevant to their station in life! A broader conception of relevance prevailed, however, and the range of school subjects was extended steadily. The latter part of the nineteenth century witnessed a widespread interest in the addition of 'manual training' to the school curriculum, whilst the twentieth century originated the concept of the 'community school' – reforms which were seen as breaking down the barriers between life of the school and the life and work of the community at large.

Ultimately, all components of the curriculum must be justified on the ground of some kind of relevance. Relevance is taken here in the narrower sense of relating the design of basic schooling to the life and work of the wider community. Relevance of this kind may be justified from several perspectives: on educational grounds as facilitating deeper contact between the child and his studies or the educational process as a whole, a learning-centred perspective; on more psychological grounds, as an aid to the socialisation of the child – an aim shared with different emphases by child-centred educators, the government of rigidly stratified societies and the governments of countries seeking to lessen the incidence of social stratification; and also on economic or utilitarian grounds – as permitting the transfer of useful knowledge and skills to the younger generation or to the population as a whole (with benefits to the individual student and to society generally). As will be indicated throughout this book, society-centred aims – building the stability and skills of the nation – have featured strongly in the advocacy of work-related and community-related school programmes. It is this focus that has sometimes tended to weaken programme design – an issue to which attention is also drawn throughout the book.

Relevance Through Work-experience Programmes: A Historical Perspective

Before the advent of the school as a mass institution, children were introduced to the life skills of their home communities through regular person-to-person contact – father and son, mother and daughter, child and neighbour. 'They learned by living and doing. In the homes and on the farms they were taught the skills of the society, and the behaviour expected of its members. They learned the kind of grasses which were suitable for which purposes, the work which had to be done on the crops, or the care which had to be given to animals, by joining with their elders in this work' (Nyerere 1967:2). The impact of formal schooling in the nineteenth and twentieth centuries destroyed much of this natural learning process.

Many people have not regarded this as a problem, viewing the spread of literacy as of value in itself, the spread of schooling as a step toward greater social equity, or the institution of 'school' as just one of the many new institutions appropriate to the times. Others have felt dissatisfaction with the situation in which children have been assigned primarily to bookwork during the years when their physical competencies first come to fruition and when their natural curiosity and interest in concrete activities could have led them to build up practical skills and experience – experience of the basic processes of life support, for example.

It is useful to glance briefly at the debate and experiments in work-related schooling in nineteenth-century Europe and America before moving on to a discussion of programmes in the countries of the Third World. Europe and America at that time had some of the characteristics of the contemporary Third World – in particular newly growing systems of mass formal education, widespread poverty and endemic destitution. In addition the ideas which educational administrators developed regarding mass education in these countries were exported almost immediately to Africa and Asia, through Christian missions and colonial governments, and form part of the historical experience of Third World countries themselves.[2]

Nineteenth-century Europe

The earliest European initiatives were those of child-centred educators – whose concern was as much to round out the educational experience of the child as to convey vocationally useful knowledge and skills. Rousseau and his disciples explored this approach. Rousseau suggested in *Emile* that a private tutor should introduce even the child of a rich man to the work of farmers in their fields and of artisans in their workshops. He should also, suggested Rousseau, convey a specialised knowledge of one particular trade such as carpentry through joint apprenticeship of tutor and pupil to a practising craftsman on a part-time basis. Pestalozzi ran a small school where pauper children were educated through craftwork as well as book studies.[3] His colleague, de Fellenburg, set up two schools with an agriculturally-biased curriculum – an expensive one for the sons of the rich and a work school for the sons of the poor, both of which attracted visitors from all over Europe. In the UK, Lord Brougham persistently drew the attention of the public to these experiments, and in the 1820s and 1830s experiments similar to de Fellenburg's agricultural Poor School took place in rural Sussex, on Lady Byron's estate at Ealing, and elsewhere.[4]

Froebel established his own basically religious philosophy of education after earlier experiences in a Pestalozzi-style school. He drew up plans for a school in which the afternoons would be devoted to productive work in the field, the forest, the school workshop and the house.[5]

Sloyd handwork, based on Froebel, generated a great deal of interest in the United Kingdom and Europe, with annual pilgrimages of teachers from 1884 on to attend courses organised by Salomon in Sweden.

Further initiatives towards work-related schooling resulted from the concern of policy-makers and opinion leaders over the social and economic problems of the times. In the United Kingdom, there were some early experiments with 'schools of industry' where the products of pupils' labour were used to defray the costs of basic schooling. Later Dr Kay-Shuttleworth was moved by his experience as an Assistant Poor Law Commissioner to develop a model urban school and a model rural teacher training college in which craft and agricultural work played a key role. A major objective was to provide craft training to pauper children who would otherwise have been tempted towards anti-social activities, such as petty thievery. He also sought to establish the social order through building up pride in skilled work and simple living. As secretary to the first British policy-making body for education, the Committee of the Privy Council on Education founded in 1839, Kay-Shuttleworth, perhaps influenced by studies of de Fellenburg's work, recommended that the village school should become a focal point of community life and instituted grants in respect of school gardens, workshops, kitchens and wash-houses.

The focus of concern shifted later in the century with the development of international competition in the industrial sphere. Both in the United Kingdom and the United States trade exhibitions gave an impetus to the idea of 'manual training' in schools as a means of keeping up in the industrial race. In the United Kingdom, the Great Exhibition of 1851, followed by the evidence of the 1867 Exhibition in Paris, led to the idea that Britain's economic position was threatened for lack of technical education. Manuals for 'hand and eye' training were prepared in the 1880s and in 1895 the Department of Education tried to make this 'manual training' compulsory in primary schools, but withdrew compulsion because teachers found the work too difficult. In the same period, schools were offered grants to assist in establishing workshops for training older boys. The 'hand and eye' theory underlying these initiatives was that the brain centre connected with the hand was developed between the first and fourteenth year of life and that neglect of handwork of this period might undermine the reservoirs of craft skill at the service of the nation. The 'manual training' group, gathered around Philip Magnus, principal of the City and Guilds Institute, was independent of the Sloyd groups mentioned earlier, each party holding separate examinations and publishing separate magazines.

The administrative class which sought to provide work-oriented schooling for the workers in Britain sought also to provide the same kind of schooling in overseas territories such as Australia, New Zealand, West Africa and the West Indies (Graham 1971:61). A Select Committee of Parliament noted with disquiet in 1842 that no efforts had been made to offer agricultural instruction in the schools of West Africa and recommended that governments and missions should remedy this deficiency. Dr Madden, a special Commissioner who had inspected the schools in 1841, observed that schools operated at the level of words, with little attention to things, thinking or 'instruction in the habits of industry'. The situation attracted the attention of Kay-Shuttleworth, and a report drafted by him and submitted by the Privy Council to the Colonial Office gave suggestions for the establishment of 'industrial schools' in the colonies. The report expressed the desirability of more detailed knowledge of local conditions and in the absence of this, its prescriptions read very much as if designed to fit Kay-Shuttleworth's formula for social uplift through elementary schools in Britain – teaching about diet, cleanliness, ventilation, clothing, agriculture and handicrafts. The turn of the century saw much concern about an agricultural bias to the curriculum in India and a concern for 'hand and eye' and agricultural training in West Africa.

Two further streams of thought on the subject of work and schooling originated in nineteenth-century Europe. Marx and Engels sought a revolutionary solution to the sufferings of the labouring classes, and a post-revolutionary educational system in which proletarian consciousness would be enhanced through combining education with productive labour and through ensuring a close relationship between schools and the productive units of society. These ideas were to re-emerge in the twentieth century with the labour schools initiated by Lenin and with later initiatives in the USSR and in other socialist states.

Yet another response to the social, economic and technological changes of the nineteenth century was to regard them as degrading the quality of life for all. Ruskin, Morris and others despaired at the disappearance of the traditional craftsman and at the confinement of unfortunate millions to airless factories and polluted towns. The Fellowship of the New Life, a neo-Ruskinite group, was founded in 1883 to seek the regeneration of society through new styles of community living based on traditional modes of production, and spiritual rather than material fulfilment. The Fellowship sought a new approach to education and led to the foundation of a series of private schools in Britain and Europe in which manual work was included as an experience in its own right. Thus, Abbotsholme, opened in Derbyshire in 1889, provided for agriculture, gardening, the care of animals, carpentry, carving, metalwork and other crafts, while tailoring, boot-making and cooking also featured in the original plans but were not actually introduced (Stewart 1968). This neo-Ruskinite impulse was to influence Gandhi whose first involvement in education was the schooling of labourers' children at Tolstoy Farm in South Africa. There, schooling consisted of farmwork, housework and craft activities in the morning and ordinary school studies in the afternoon. (See Gandhi 1927, and Fischer 1951.)

Nineteenth-century America

The fear of international competition as well as concern over urban social unrest led to the development of a manual training programme in America concurrent with developments in Europe. The Philadelphia Centennial Exposition of 1876 included a display of formal workshop instruction developed at the Moscow Imperial Technical School. This led John Runkle at Massachusetts Institute of Technology and Calvin Woodward at Washington University, St Louis, to set up manual-training high schools combining traditional subjects with woodwork and metalwork. They then called for an extension of manual training to the schools at large, and encountered a favourable response. Despite changes in form and name this impulse continued to influence the pattern of schooling thereafter.[6]

Further south, the needs of the slaves newly freed after the American civil war, generated another initiative in work-oriented studies. Samuel Chapman Armstrong, raised as the son of a missionary educator in Hawaii, acquainted with the problems of black Americans by the civil war, and further sensitised to these problems by work as administrative agent for Virginia of the Freedman's Bureau, decided to devote his life to building up an educational institute similar to an industrial school he had seen in Hawaii as a child. In 1868 he established Hampton Institute in Hampton, Virginia, set in 160 acres of land. This institute sought to combine schooling and work and thereby to prepare black students for work as teachers, or as model craftsmen and cultivators among their own communities. Armstrong's method was to combine ordinary schooling with work in the farm, workshops or housework departments. 'The needle, the broom and the wash-tub, the awl, the plane and the plough, became the allies of the globe, the blackboard and the textbook', he noted. To further his overriding objective of the development of character, he also added military drill (without arms), military-style uniforms, and daily inspections of persons and rooms (Peabody 1918). The charisma of Armstrong led his pupil, and subsequently his assistant, Booker T. Washington, to devote a lifetime to propagating the same educational doctrines. Nominated by Armstrong to head a new industrial education venture at Tuskegee, Alabama, Washington at first had difficulty in convincing his pupils (selected as being over 16 and literate) of the educational value of working to establish and develop the school farm. For several years, many new arrivals at Tuskegee bore notes from their parents asking that they be taught 'book learning' but not be required to do practical work. Following the Hampton precedent, however, all students were expected to do manual work, and respect the virtues of the toothbrush, bathtub, shoe polish and punctuality.

Both institutes undertook extension work among the rural community and Tuskegee was doubly fortunate in this respect. Its founder had discovered the people's needs by going from door to door and staying in their tiny cabins, while personally recruiting his first intake of students through a tour of the district. Later Tuskegee attracted the services of George Washington Carver, the agricultural scientist who turned down offers of employment from leading industrialists to continue with his work of developing new crops and improved agricultural practices in the South.[7] In this rare instance, an agriculturalist of the first rank was fully committed to the task of discovering an improved peasant agriculture which an educational institution could help diffuse among the people.

Despite domestic opposition, the Hampton-Tuskegee model gained international acclaim. In particular, the model was strongly recommended at the first World Missionary Conference held at Edinburgh in 1910 and from then on there was a constant stream of foreign visitors, principally missionaries, to the American South. Later, the model was adopted by the Phelps-Stokes Commissions of 1920-1 and 1924, headed by Dr Jesse Jones, a Welshman who had taught social Darwinism at Hampton. Dr Jones also won the Colonial Office in London to his way of thinking, with the consequence that British administrators attempted to impose the Hampton-Tuskegee approach on their African colonies from the 1920s on.[8] The Americans likewise exported 'industrial education' to the Philippines as the basis of the school system established there in 1901.

The Twentieth Century – The Colonial Period

Some countries have experienced a succession of colonial impulses towards work-oriented schooling. In India, in the late nineteenth century and the first decade of the present century the development of separate curricula for rural schools occurred in several provinces. The rural schools placed more emphasis on indigenous systems of arithmetic and accounting and on agriculturally relevant topics, as well as providing for gardening or farmwork. They became highly unpopular and were finally dropped, because rural families wished their children to qualify for the opportunities in higher schooling and government service open to children who had followed the more orthodox urban school curricula. But while the Department of Education in 1920 expressed sympathy with peasants who wanted the schools to concentrate on bookwork, the late 1920s and 1930s again saw official pressure towards an agricultural bias, especially in the 'vernacular middle school'.[9]

In Ceylon, likewise, there were recurrent official efforts to stimulate 'relevant' education in rural schools. These had little impact until the 1930s when one administrator, R. Patrick, attempted to create agricultural and other programmes at several hundred rural schools with post-primary classes. The programme faded into obscurity with his departure (Jayasuriya 1969:96-7). In the Philippines many revisions of the primary and intermediate school curricula took place, each, however, providing for handwork or 'industrial work', the study of hygiene etc., on the best Hampton-Tuskegee principles (Fresnova and Casim 1964: 159-78).

The early experiences of West Africa in this respect have already been noted. While Madden and Kay-Shuttleworth made immediate impact, legislation was passed in the 1880s providing for the establishment of industrial schools in Sierra Leone and the Gold Coast. Governor Rodger of the Gold Coast, returning from a visit to the southern United State, set up a committee in 1908 'to revise educational rules, to establish a training institution for teachers, to establish a technical school, and to introduce hand and eye, industrial and agricultural training into the schools'. A number of schools operated on these lines in the pre-1914 period and the trend was reinforced in the 1920s when Governor Guggisberg's own 'applied' orientation as an engineer found confirmation as an approach to schooling in his discussions with members of the Phelps-Stokes Commission to Africa of 1920-1 (Foster 1965). Governor Cameron of Tanganyika also attempted to promote the concept of locally adapted education as appropriate to the 'indirect rule' policy of the 1920s (Listowel 1965, Cameron and Dodd 1970). In Kenya, the pressure of white settlers had led to a strictly Hampton-Tuskegee approach to African schooling. From its inception, the Education Department had taken *Working with the Hands* by Booker T. Washington as its principal inspiration and African pupils were indentured for trade studies during the last three years of schooling. The deliberate restriction of educational and economic opportunities for Kenyan Africans ensured a poor response to the school gardens programme of the 1920s, when some such gardens were destroyed; and the programme for training 'Jeanes' visiting teachers (a transplant from Hampton and Tuskegee) to relate village schooling more closely to local needs and activities, operated in a fairly unreceptive environment partly for the same reason.[10]

Among other such projects there were two noteworthy attempts to introduce contemporary educational thought into a Muslim context. Hans Vischer, later secretary of the British Advisory Committee on Education in the Colonies, worked in Northern Nigeria to train Koranic teachers in the use of newly devised, locally relevant Hausa textbooks, and to build a vocational element into the curriculum (Graham 1966). Later V.L. Griffiths, as founder-principal of the rural Bakht er Ruda training college in the Sudan, tried to combine a child-centred approach and a rural orientation in his programme of textbook development, in-service and pre-service teacher training. Griffiths took pains constantly to review his objectives in the light of experience, and, in consequence, moved towards a narrower range of objectives better adapted to the resource endowments of the schools and to the aspirations of their pupils and hence more likely of fulfilment (Griffiths 1975).

Of later colonial initiatives, the 1950s school agriculture programme in Tanganyika is the best documented and features as a case-study in Chapter 2.

Third World Initiatives

Policy-makers in a number of independent Third World countries have echoed the experience of nineteenth-century Europe and America and the exhortations of colonial administrations and have urged the desirability of bringing together the world of school and the world of the surrounding community. The rationale offered is expressed in different terms, and often refers to the need to develop a nationally relevant programme to supersede schooling designed to meet the requirements of a colonial power. Problems of rural poverty and of prematurely rising levels of expectation regarding material security and prosperity among school-leavers have been predominant among the reasons given for including work experience in the new curriculum. Offsetting costs through pupil labour has also featured in some schemes.

Gandhian 'Basic National Education' constitutes one of the most striking examples of a nationalist venture treading ground earlier explored by colonial administrators with only limited success.

President Nyerere's 1967 initiative in proposing 'education for self-reliance' in Tanzania represents a more contemporary and

Africanised version of what Gandhi hoped for. Again the idea of productive work as the key to the personal as well as the intellectual development of the pupil forms a basic element in an integrated approach to a nationally valid schooling. As in Basic Education, the association of this initiative with the person of a statesman internationally respected for his integrity and philosophy gives it an added force.

A different situation underlaid the programmes for relevant rural education developed in Mexico in the 1920s and 1930s and in Turkey in the 1940s. In each case a reformist government of a long independent state sought to remedy the almost total absence of rural educational provision by the creation of a school network aligned to the needs of the rural areas. (See Chapter 2.)

There have been many other government-sponsored programmes. A recent survey of eleven Asian countries indicated that 'work-oriented education' was provided for at both the first and second level of schooling in each.[11] In some cases, however, the response was more indicative of government aspiration than of actual conditions in the schools. Asian programmes cited in the course of the chapters which follow include the work-experience programmes developed in some parts of India as a sequel to Gandhian Basic education; the schoolchildren's paddy-weeding campaigns in Ceylon in the late 1960s; and the pre-vocational studies programme launched in Sri Lanka in 1972 and terminated in 1977. Besides these government-sponsored programmes there have also been initiatives arising on a decentralised basis. A notable example was the Philippines 'community school' programme, which sprang from the discovery that schools could contribute something positive to the task of local reconstruction after the 1939-45 war. The initiative came first from the Association of Philippine School Superintendents; government support followed thereafter. (See Chapter 2.) The same was true of the vocationally oriented 'barrio high school' movement launched by Dr Pedro Orata. The movement spread to other parts of the Philippines and barrio high schools finally obtained a government charter. Another noteworthy venture arose from a different strategy. A range of agricultural and other projects were initiated in the schools adjacent to the Pakistan – now Bangladesh – Academy of Rural Development at Comilla, as part of the Academy's more general studies of new approaches to integrated rural development.[12]

There has been considerable support in Africa also for the inclusion of work activities in the school programme, though rarely as emphatically as in Tanzania. The post-primary 'colleges of rural education' in Guinea, ruralised education in Cameroon, ruralisation of schooling in the Malagasy Republic, the 'continuation' programme in selected middle schools in Ghana, and pilot ventures based on teacher training colleges in Uganda, Sierra Leone and elsewhere[13] are prominent models.

In Latin America, governments have shown a continuing interest in the potential of community-oriented schooling to uplift deprived rural populations. A system of nuclear and satellite schools was developed in Bolivia in 1933, adopted soon thereafter in Peru and Ecuador, and recently revived in Peru and the Dominican Republic. According to this system, specialist workers trained in agricultural extension, health, literacy and work and community organisation were attached to the central school and travelled to outpost schools to train teachers in community work. The Andean Indian programme co-ordinated by the ILO functioned in a similar fashion. 'Production schools', recently introduced in Panama, derive from this tradition. The 'schools to the countryside' and basic 'secondary schools in the countryside', developed by the government of Cuba, represent a different approach, in which the problems of providing substantial work-experience programmes for a large population of urban schoolchildren have been overcome through the investment of managerial and physical resources on a scale commensurate with policy commitments to this ideal.[14]

A different model is illustrated by initiatives taken by individual schools. The Mayflower School in Nigeria, van Rensburg's experiments in Botswana, the Above Rocks School in Jamaica, and Litowa School in Tanzania constitute but the documented tip of an iceberg of individual ventures throughout the Third World through which school and work or school and community have been brought closer together.[15]

The Provision of Work Opportunities in Childhood: A First Review

This brief review of initiatives in work-related schooling shows up some striking contrasts. As proposed in early-nineteenth-century England, for example, it was conceived as a way of keeping the members of the lower classes fully orientated towards their menial lot – at a time when members of the middle and upper classes were often unwilling to see the masses literate at all. Kay-Shuttleworth in the mid-century, though educationally progressive, also thought in terms of keeping the working classes contented with their place in society. At the same time Marx and Engels were recommending work experience in post-revolutionary schools as a means of raising the degree of proletarian consciousness of the working population. Armstrong's and

Washington's craft-centred programmes in America were designed to prepare Southern blacks, newly freed from slavery, to occupy with dignity the humble positions in small-scale agriculture, craftwork and domestic service that were all that was open to them. That was not so very much different from the new approach to education at Abbotsholme, intended for the sons of the 'directing classes' of imperial England. Woodwork and metalwork in schools were promoted as much by the protagonists of industrial progress (Magnus and Woodward) as by the neo-Ruskinites (Abbotsholme and its successors and, to an extent, Gandhi). Education in craftwork and agriculture was promoted by colonial governments in an attempt to stabilise the colonial situation and has been adopted by independent Third World governments as a way of overcoming the attitudes associated with pre-independence educational structures. Work-experience programmes have been introduced by governments of the right, the centre and the left, colonial and autonomous.

Two hypotheses may be suggested to interpret the apparent paradox. First, certain educators and policy-makers feel as a matter of intuitive judgement that practical activities add 'balance' to the experience of schooling – or that work activities add a necessary dimension to the experience of growing up – and that this balance will benefit the students themselves in respect of their personal development, and therefore, in one way or another, will also benefit society as a whole. This kind of reasoning is equally applicable in varied political contexts. Second, there has been a recurrent tendency for policy-makers and opinion-leaders to look hopefully to schools as agencies which could contribute to the solution of the social and economic problems of the times, whatever they believe these to be.

In the case of problems such as rural backwardness or unemployment or unrest among the 'educated unemployed', the suggestion has readily arisen that the schools should convey vocational or pre-vocational knowledge and skills and also attitudes favourable to manual work. In most instances, concern for the solution of social and economic problems has been dominant in the rationale offered for the introduction of work-experience programmes. It is possible, however, that a natural impulse towards providing children with practical experience of the basic processes of life support has contributed even to the formulation of programmes justified mainly in terms of social and economic issues. There appears to be a tendency to believe that work-oriented schooling offers ready solutions to socio-economic problems, a view that Foster *et alia* have vigorously denounced as the vocational-school fallacy.[16]

Relevance Through Experience Relating to Other Aspects of Community Life

A second persistent theme in relevant education has stressed that the school should be brought together with its parent community. In England the impact of Kay-Shuttleworth's philosophy was blunted by the emphasis on basic communication skills fostered by the system of 'payment by results'. The community dimension was not revived until the twentieth century, with the 'village colleges' introduced by Morris in Cambridgeshire in the 1920s and 1930s. By the 1960s a new generation of 'community schools' had emerged, characterised especially by the attempt to stimulate community use of the resources, human and physical, of the school. At the same time, a more general movement towards locally oriented studies resulted from the introduction of 'Mode III' examinations at secondary level, with school-designed programmes examined internally but moderated externally.

In the United States, the community dimension had been a feature of the Institutes at Hampton and Tuskegee. The Phelps-Stokes reports give a vivid account of the mobile schools sent out from Tuskegee to offer instruction in agricultural techniques, home management etc., and farmer conferences were held at the college. The Jeanes teachers based at Hampton and Tuskegee likewise sought to raise the degree of community orientation in the rural elementary schools – encouraging teachers to extend the influence of the schools into the neighbourhood and set up parents' leagues and boys' and girls' clubs to develop 'healthful recreation'. The inter-war period saw a widespread interest in the concept of the 'community school', again concentrated mainly in the depressed rural South. The characteristics of the community school as it developed in America have been summarised as follows:

> *First*: The students and teachers use the resources of the community as the core of the curriculum, relating the major content of the curriculum to what is happening and can be studied in the community.
> *Second*: The school is used, not only by children, but by the adults of the community, serving as a community centre, a place for adult education and recreation, a focal point for the community.
> *Third*: The teachers are full participating members of the community, with the children, and carry out projects of community development. These projects are part of the academic activities of the school, but

> they also bring together the children and the adults of the community to act on mutually agreed community problems and improvement projects.[17]

Activities included school lunch programmes, co-operative harvesting machinery, co-operative canneries, craft rooms for women, and so on. There was some limited research evidence that standards of performance in respect of the orthodox school subjects compared favourably with performance in control schools following orthodox curricula.

In the colonial era, schools under British and American influence were encouraged to adopt the community orientation of Hampton and Tuskegee. Dr Jesse Jones, chairman of the Phelps-Stokes Commissions, prescribed a formula for education in Africa based on his experience at Hampton. The schools should, he believed, focus their attention on the key areas of health and sanitation, appreciation and use of the environment, home and household, and recreation – physical, intellectual and spiritual.[18] These recommendations were taken up by the British Advisory Committee on Education in the Colonies, set up in 1923, and led to the philosophy of locally adapted education which British educators sought to introduce in Africa during the remainder of the colonial period. 'Adapted' education included health studies and community service projects as well as agriculture and craftwork. When, however, Mumford attempted a truly 'adapted' education at Malangali School in the Tanganyika of the 1920s, the Christian missions were horrified at his attempt to build upon tribal traditions and the experiment was short-lived.[19] Graduates from the Jeanes School, at Kabete in Kenya, made valiant efforts in the field of locally adapted community education, including the development of localised versions of the Boy Scout movement (King 1971 a).

Community uplift was an integral part of the movements towards relevant rural education in independent states also – in the Mexico of the 1920s and 1930s, and in the Turkey of the late 1930s and 1940s. In both instances the schoolteacher was expected to fulfil a dual role, that of teacher in the orthodox sense and that of community development worker. The 'community schools' movement in the 'decolonised' Philippines in the late 1940s and early 1950s, did not have any specific blueprint. Most schools, however, engaged in community service activities, including many health-related projects, and many teachers took on the additional roles of community development worker and adult literacy tutor.

In more recent times, President Nyerere has been one of the

foremost advocates of the community dimension in schooling, calling on the schools of Tanzania to prepare students for their future role as self-reliant citizens in a state dedicated to socialism, equality and individual freedom. The 'community education centres' underline the primacy of school - community integration by grouping various community facilities (workshops, dispensary, co-operative shop and stores, day-care centre for children, post office, bank etc.) on the same campus as the school. A curriculum development group based at Korogwe College of National Education and Kwamsisi community school has further explored in detail the possibilities of a community oriented curriculum. Under this scheme pupils follow a course of study in which only mathematics, Swahili, English and political education are taught as separate subjects and the remaining subjects are organised around topics and projects with local as well as general relevance.[20] The curriculum reform programme in Cameroon likewise relied heavily on the theme of environmental studies as providing for an approach to local relevance (Lallez 1974). Curriculum development work at Bunumbu and elsewhere in Sierra Leone has a similar focus (Hawes 1976). Curriculum development for primary and junior secondary pupils in general has a built-in dynamic towards environmental studies in various guises, with the emphasis on project work and investigation by pupils as well as pressures to help pupils understand their nation's problems.

Structure of the Analysis

This chapter has revealed a large number of attempts at 'relevant' education in a large number of countries. Examining them for lessons and guidelines is made difficult by the almost universal lack of complete and reliable information. In particular, while statements of objectives and plans are relatively plentiful, systematic histories of development and outcomes are not. Accordingly, Chapter 2 offers six case-studies, for which good documentation is available. Chapter 3 reviews the stated objectives of a number of relevance programmes – finding them unrealistic in scope and not easily susceptible to measurement. The underlying reasons for various programmes are studied in Chapter 4. Thereafter, the focus shifts to the management of education innovations: what conceptual approaches might have been adopted (Chapter 5) and what pragmatic steps actually were put in train (Chapters 6 to 9). The final chapter evaluates what alternatives of policy are available to educators interested in 'relevant' education.

Notes

1. See UNESCO (1969).
2. See for example, Anderson (1970), Morrison (1976), Foster (1965a).
3. See Heafford (1967 : 78-83).
4. For historical material on the United Kingdom see Smith (1931) and Stewart and McCann (1967 : 136-69).
5. See Annotation to Froebel (1887 : 37-8) by the translator, W.N. Hailmann.
6. See Lazerson and Grubb (1976 : 2-17, 60-6). The authors note that 'By the end of the nineteenth century few students would pass through the American education system without some exposure to manual work.'
7. See Spencer (1955). For a brief review of Washington Carver's agricultural work, see Tompkins and Bird (1974).
8. See King (1971a) for a historical review of the Hampton-Tuskegee model in Africa.
9. See Nurullah and Naik (1951); and also the *Quinquennial Review of the Progress of Education in India, 1917-1922* (Government of India), pp. 121-2, and Hartog (1939 : 38).
10. For particulars of the Kenya initiatives see King (1971ab) and Kenya Education Department Reports from 1924 to 1938. See also Sinclair (1976a).
11. See the report of a seminar, held in Tokyo in 1975, on 'Curriculum development for work-oriented education'; published jointly by the UNESCO Regional Office for Education in Asia, Bangkok and the National Institute for Educational Research of Japan.
12. See Solaiman (1975).
13. See for example, Ponsioen (1972), King (1976), Lallez (1974) and Boakye (1976).
14. Particulars of the recent initiatives in Panama and Peru are taken from Lourié (1976) and Bizot (1975) respectively.
15. See Houghton and Tregear (1969).
16. Foster (1965b).
17. Cited from the review by Weeks. See also Havighurst and Neugarten (1962) and Olsen (1963).
18. See the Phelps-Stokes Commission reports (Jones 1922, 1925) and Jones's statement of his general philosophy of education (Jones 1926).
19. See Lewis (1954), Cameron and Dodd (1970) and Morrison (1976) for brief notes on the school, and Mcrris-Hale (1969) for further particulars.
20. See for example, Moshi (1976) and Nimpuno (1976), and – for the report of a workshop on implementation – Mwobahe and Mbilinyi (1975).

2 SIX CASE-STUDIES FROM THE HISTORY OF RELEVANCE EDUCATION*

Certain programmes of relevance education are amenable to study. They also happen to have each made a major impact on their respective national systems of schooling, even though they have subsequently been terminated or have faded from view. They comprise:

- Mexico's Rural Schools
- Turkey's Village Institutes
- Gandhian Basic Education in India
- the Philippines Community Schools
- the 1950s Tanganyika Agricultural Programme
- Rural Education Centres in Upper Volta.

The aim here is to give an account of the origin and development of each programme and indicate how its history fits the analysis of alternative strategies presented later. Hence the 'review of strategy' in each case covers in turn the question of the broad strategy for change, the type of innovation envisaged at school level, innovation systems for educators and for ancillary research and development work, responsiveness of the schools' clients to the innovation within the schools, and responsiveness of educators to the demands placed upon them.

Mexico's Rural Schools

Origins and Overt Objectives[1]

Rural education in Mexico had been totally neglected prior to 1910. The fall of Porfirio Diaz in that year led to the founding of a few primitive rural schools, but the onset of a decade of intermittent revolutionary war brought them to a halt. Meanwhile, however, the peasants demanded, as their highest priorities, land reform and rural schools. Provision for free schooling was built into the constitution of 1917, and under President Obregon (1921-4) the federal government initiated a rural school programme. José Vasconcelos, architect of the programme, was a Catholic humanist.[2] 'His education was a moral crusade, upholding platonic ideas, stressing the 3 Rs, and scorning Deweyites and American pedagogy in general. Distrustful of what was new in education, he found his inspiration in the ancient Greeks and in the friars of the Conquest' (Ruiz 1963: 27). The latter had placed emphasis on educating the Indians in practical skills as well as religious doctrine, and Vasconcelos saw the need for such a dual emphasis in the twentieth century also. He believed that the school should educate children and adults alike: they should encompass 'work' and 'the community'.

In the 1920s the objective of education in practical skills was to help rural folk through crafts, new agricultural techniques, and measures relating to health. Vasconcelos's successors, Saenz and Ramires, differed in educational philosophy (they were ardent supporters of Dewey) but agreed that rural schools should be concerned with 'the social and economic betterment of the masses', and should become Schools of Action. Narciso Bassols, Education Minister 1931-4, a socialist planner, was less interested in the classics of Dewey and more concerned with practical skills. 'A hungry Indian cannot be turned into a good scholar, and, furthermore, his studies only have value in so far as they aid him completely to transform his economic life.' Instead of an education for the individual, he prescribed 'economic education of the whole nucleus of the peasant population considered as units' (Ruiz 1963: 51).

Rural education emerged as the intended complement of land reforms, providing knowledge and skills to the newly liberated peons, under President Cardenas (1934-40) who took a personal interest in rural schools. Learning, productive work, and social action were to be linked more closely than before, and the ideals of the revolution and of socialist planning to be taught explicitly. At the same time, Cardenas lifted restrictions on the curricula of rural schools and gave them parity of status with urban schools. This reform was all that remained from 1940 on, when succeeding presidents reacted against two decades of anti-clerical rural schooling and the policy of using the schools as a platform for the spread of socialist thinking.

Programme Development

Vasconcelos began in 1921 by getting together a group of (urban) volunteers, termed 'missionaries', willing to organise the programme in the countryside:

> From village to village they went, by horseback, mule, or on foot, spreading the idea and awakening the people to the need for education. They organised hundreds of schools in the villages, humble and elementary, but schools nevertheless, training teachers for them from among the local population . . . La Casa del Pueblo, the House of the People . . . was for everyone, on the theory that education

> must minister to all lest the neglect of the adults hinder the learning of the child. The children came during the day, the adults at night . . . Learning to read and write the Spanish Language, simple arithmetic, a few fundamentals of geography and national history: this was the academic curriculum. The vocational side was elementary. To give as much as possible to students who would seldom go beyond the fourth year of school was the objective. (Ruiz 1963:37.)

The School of Action which followed reinforced the initial concern with social relevance. Visits from doctors and nurses were encouraged, wells were dug for pure water, and the open-air theatre was enlisted in the fight against alcoholism. A vigorous programme of expansion was set in motion: by 1931 the number of rural schools had risen to 6,796. (The latter figure may be compared, however, with the 58,000 or so communities of under 4,000 population which had no school.) This achievement represented substantial community commitment, since the government supplied only teachers and a minimum of books and paper: the community had to provide school, furniture and equipment.

Nevertheless, many peasants were too poor or otherwise demoralised to benefit. Less than a third of school-age children were said to enrol in school, and attendance was poor also (about one-third of registered pupils never attended). In the 1920s, some 98 per cent of pupils left school before completing their studies, mostly during the first two years.

Even so, some schools achieved vigorous programmes of child and adult education, with activities in fields such as agriculture, handicrafts, sports and health. In contrast, many schools, confronted by the harshness of the environment, failed to take on these wider functions:

> Poorly equipped, understaffed, their activities isolated one from another, the Schools of Action lacked realistic emphasis. Their work relied almost entirely on the enthusiasm and goodwill of community, students, and teachers, which did not take the place of training or substitute for a coherent, comprehensive programme of rural reform. 'The intent is excellent' wrote Gruening. 'But in practice as I observed it, there was little else than the old routine teaching – of the three Rs, geography, national history, with one child reciting while fifty were non-participant'. The immediate needs of the community were ignored. Less than half of the schools cultivated vegetable gardens or raised chickens, only 12 per cent kept bees, less than 14 per cent raised rabbits, nearly 55 per cent had no classes in arts and crafts, and, despite the emphasis on thrift, more than 70 per cent had no savings

banks. (Ruiz 1963 : 42.)

Whatever the gloom of this account, it remains clear that the proportions of schools which **did** manage to approximate some of the ideals were not negligible.

The 1930s saw an increase in the pace of constructing new rural schools, and a new emphasis on the role of the teacher in social action. The co-operative was introduced, initially as a means of raising funds needed for schooling, later as a means of resolving community problems. By 1940, over 800 co-operatives had been organised. But often the teacher ran foul of the local middleman who activated his political contacts to the teacher's disadvantage. It may be noted that even where integrated development programmes were planned, there was disappointment at the peasants' response. 'In the Laguna region, for instance, scene of Mexico's greatest experiment with collectivised agriculture, out of a school age population of 28,621, only 15,335 on average attended classes, much of the loss being due to lack of parental interest' (Ruiz 1963 : 63). On the one hand it was felt that schools without land reform and basic services were almost a waste; on the other, some two-thirds of the *ejidos* (traditional-style collective land holdings) established by 1940 lacked a school *of any kind.*

The whole concept of the rural school as having special functions and *modus operandi* was abandoned by the conservative administrations of the 1940s and, perhaps significantly, Vasconcelos, 'morose and disillusioned', accepted a post as adviser to Vejar Vasquez, the Education Minister who in the early 1940s brought the reforming era to an end.

Review of Strategy

The basic strategy was one of government command. The government supplied the rural community with a literate person as teacher and with a minimum of books and paper. The community was expected to supply land, buildings, equipment and other inputs, so that teacher and community together could develop a programme of relevant schooling. There was little the government could do to enforce this broader concept of schooling, however, and attention came to be focused in practice more on the work of the 'cultural missions' and pre-service rural teacher training.

The type of activity required of the schools was defined in flexible terms. The systems for teacher induction were carefully designed to help teachers devise locally adapted programmes. Vasconcelos's first 75 'missionaries' were graduates of the urban teacher training schools and university, who had experienced the hardships of rural life when fighting for the revolution. They initiated the rural schools movement by travelling through the countryside, persuading the *campesinos* to build a school and provide land for training. The missionaries would then select a literate local person and train him for his work as a teacher. These missionaries were soon fully occupied with administrative work and their teacher training function was taken up by the 'cultural missions'. The first of these was assembled in 1923 on an *ad hoc* basis to offer guidance to recently appointed teachers in Hidalgo district. Ramirez was director and pedagogue, and was assisted by a soap-maker, a tanner, a physician, an expert on farming and a teacher of folk songs. The second mission to Morelos, had two agronomists, a carpenter and a home economics teacher. These missionaries were selected for their practical skills and dedication, rather than their formal qualifications.

This led to an unexpected response on the part of local inhabitants to the activities of the teacher training mission. At Hidalgo the men took an especial interest in the budding of fruit trees, while at Morelos, the local women manifested interest in the home economics programme. 'From these chance developments a close relationship was formed between the mission and the community. Eventually the community became the focus of the mission's programme, where the teachers of the surrounding villages under the guidance of the missionaries found solutions for scores of village problems by solving the one they had before them, and where the people learned to help themselves by cooperating with their teachers' (Ruiz 1963 : 92).

The first cultural mission lasted three weeks which was felt to be too brief. By 1932 the schedule had been lengthened to four months, with the first ten weeks devoted to preliminary work in the local community before the teachers arrived. The number of teacher trainees was limited to 50, to permit individual attention.

A government study in 1933 nevertheless concluded that the overall programme had been 'thinly spread and weakly enacted'. To remedy this, the missions were for a time made non-travelling and attached to the Regional Peasant Schools set up by Bassols to integrate and supersede the rural normal schools and agricultural schools. This left vast areas unprovided for, however, and President Cardenas made the missions mobile again. They were still to offer leadership in the struggle for land, and this led finally to their dissolution by President Cardenas, when national unity became paramount in the international confrontation caused by Cardenas's expropriation of the foreign-owned oil companies in 1938.

Rural teacher training schools, of which the first opened in 1922, numbered 17 a decade later. They offered a two-year programme of pre-service training for persons with four or preferably six years of primary schooling. Courses included academic subjects, pedagogy, practice teaching, agriculture, craftwork and home economics. These schools, hastily established, often lacked sufficient land and lacked the personnel and equipment required by their agricultural programme. Worse, they admitted a high proportion of urban students, contrary to the original intention, as few rural schools provided as much as four or six years of schooling. The minimum age of 16 years for boys and 14 years for girls meant that pupils could not be recruited direct from rural schools for they had left school before reaching that age. Urban trainees, on the other hand, rarely took up posts in the rural areas.

The Regional Peasant School, which superseded this earlier programme, provided for the admission of pupils aged 14 years (boys) or 12 years (girls) and offered a condensed one-year course of schooling for entrants who had not reached grade 6 previously. Proof of a rural background was also required. Trainees who wished to become teachers would follow a two-year course of teacher training after completing their two-year course in agriculture and small industries. (This reform, initiated in 1934, was thus a year or so ahead of the similar programme for the establishment of Village Institutes in Turkey.) The ten Regional Peasant Schools of 1934 increased to 33 such schools by 1940, with just over 4,000 students (spread over a four- to five-year course).[3] Though enrolments were still small in relation to needs, expansion had been too fast to permit the attainment of the standards hoped for (Ruiz 1963 : 112).

The Regional Peasant Schools were discontinued in the early 1940s, along with the special rural schools programme, and new teacher training schools were established in which there was little differentiation between the urban and rural environment.

Review of the Programme

The rural schools of the 1920s and 1930s offered a double innovation to the schools' clients. For the first time they and their children had the chance of becoming literate. They also had the opportunity to acquire practical skills disseminated through the schools. The circumstances of the times led to a real value being placed on these opportunities, even though there was little chance in the early years of children gaining formal qualifications of any kind. Literacy or some first steps towards it were perhaps especially valued. The examples of practical ventures cited in the literature suggest that not very much was added that was both new and usable – except that the *campesinos* had the opportunity in some instances to become acquainted with modern techniques of organisation through participating in school committees and programmes. There was some client motivation and it was not due to hopes of gaining government employment through completing primary schooling – few pupils completed more than a grade or two of primary school.

Teacher motivation also constituted a serious problem. An element of idealism, or satisfaction with the status of teacher, seems to have inspired the teachers recruited direct from the adult rural population – though other openings were no doubt limited. Numbers of these teachers were anxious to attend the courses provided by the 'cultural missions', and clearly some of them were committed to the broader interpretations of their duties as leaders of community development. Graduates from the extended pre-service rural teacher training courses in contrast failed to be effectively motivated towards the ideals of the rural school. The counter-pressures were too great and enforcement to use their training was evidently weak. Given the conditions obtaining in rural Mexico, graduates from the Regional Peasant Schools once appointed to rural schools promptly deserted them for appointments in the towns. Others used their qualification to gain admittance to urban schools as teachers.

In summary, the Mexican government would appear to have done what it could in years of considerable social turmoil and with a minimal budget for rural schooling. The concept of relevant schooling that was disseminated was the result of government coercion, and a substantial effort was invested in the 'cultural missions', a pioneering venture in the field of in-service training. Support was thus given to the natural innovators and those who sought actively to fulfil the role prescribed for them by the government to develop enriched programmes of community-oriented schooling. Resources and social conditions did not permit more. The concept of ongoing support for a neighbourhood group of schools, those in the vicinity of the Regional Peasant Schools, was explored briefly in 1933 but political pressures weighed in favour of providing short-term inspiration to a wider number of teachers.

The rural schools movement was itself political in origin, and developed in an era of social turmoil (the later 1920s saw feuds and bloodshed as the *Cristeros* attacked the anti-clericalism of the new schools). Its two decades of life were terminated by a change in the political complexion of the government. In Mexico certainly there was no question of community-centred education being gradually accepted, made non-political and established as a natural adjunct to the three Rs. The 1930s saw an attempt to involve the school more closely than ever in the political process, a strategy which sealed the fate of the experiment when the revolutionary spirit had spent its force.

Turkey's Village Institutes

Origins and Overt Objectives

Western education was slow to reach the villages of Turkey because educated townsfolk were unwilling to serve as teachers in the relatively inaccessible and 'backward' rural areas. The villagers likewise were unenthusiastic about Western schooling which seemed unrelated to the practicalities of rural life. The traditional *madrassas* or Koranic schools were, in contrast, highly acceptable, but Atatürk's modernist philosophy forbade the development of rural education on religious lines. Rather he wished to see the transformation of the countryside by educating children and adults in the techniques of modern, 'scientific' agriculture and crafts.

This led to two initiatives in the 1930s based on the idea of training young rural folk, who had completed their primary education, to set up schools in the rural areas – their training being focused on agriculture and other practical activities. Brief teacher training courses drawing on the facilities of state farms were initiated in 1935, and ruralised teacher training colleges proper were initiated in 1937 – both recruiting from the pool of rural youth who had completed primary schooling. The colleges, known after 1940 as Village Institutes,[4] were the brainchild of Ismail Tongua, who believed that rural youth could be more effective instruments for rural change than intellectuals imported from the cities. He advocated a course of studies incorporating topics relating to rural transformation as well as orthodox school subjects and emphasised the need for practical experience of scientific farming and craftwork. The trained teachers would thereby be encouraged to play their role of rural change agents through community education and leadership, and also by example.

The hopes invested in the new training programme are evident in the full specification of the objectives set before the Village Institute graduates:

(a) They must work to build the school (in the village where they are sent to teach), they must take care of its garden and arable land, so

> that these may be examples to the villagers; they must make the school workshop of use to the villagers; they must direct the general education and learning of the children and instruct them in health education.
> (b) On the other hand, they must raise the cultural standard of the villagers, prepare them to meet the demands of social life, direct village celebrations, introduce the villagers to the radio, put into effect various agricultural, artistic and technical projects to serve as examples to the villagers to improve both the quality and the quantity of production, see that the historic monuments are preserved, and take an active part in village life, etc. (Semin 1952 : 472.)

Programme Development

The emphasis on practical objections comes through clearly in the design of the crash courses of training initiated in 1935. These courses were attached to state model farms and most of the six or seven months training was devoted to agriculture although some general education courses were also included. After this brief training (preceded only by a four- or five-year elementary education in a rural primary school) the graduates were assigned to villages which previously had no schools. They were expected to establish schools, initiate school programmes (up to grade 3 level) for children and undertake extension work among adults. Their performance would seem to have been adequate in some sense, for the training programmes were continued from 1935 to 1946, during which time 8,675 rural youths qualified as 'instructors'. 8,543 of these taught in villages which previously had no school and a peak of 6,654 such instructors were in the schools in 1950. Some 2,500 of these instructors were still working in the schools in 1964.

Two rural teacher training colleges proper were opened on a pilot basis in 1937 and the educational legislation of 1940 provided for these institutions to be developed on a nationwide basis. There were 14 such institutions, known as Village Institutes, by the end of 1940, 20 by 1944 and 21 from 1948 on. The five-year training course (following five years of primary schooling) was to include 114 hours of general education, 58 hours of agricultural studies and 58 hours of technological studies per semester. There was no fixed syllabus initially, but in 1943 a detailed syllabus was issued under the following headings:

General Education (50% of timetable)	Hours (total over 5-year course)
Turkish	736
History	328
Geography	236
Civics	92
Mathematics	598
Physics	276
Chemistry	184
Biology	368
Foreign language	414
Penmanship	92
Painting	214
Physical education and national folklore	184
Music – instrumental and vocal	460
Military training	368
Rural economics and co-operative organisation	46

Agriculture (25% of timetable)

Fieldwork, zoo-technology, aviculture, agriculture, silkworm culture, fishing and pisciculture.

Technology (25% of timetable)

Ironwork, woodwork, masonry, mechanics, elements of electricity, and (for women) housework, child care, etc.

Incentives for students to address themselves to this formidable programme of work included provision for the most talented students to proceed to study at the secondary lycées and at university, and government fellowships for studies overseas. They also had access to the Institute of Higher Education founded in 1942 to train teacher educators for the Village Institutes. The Institute of Higher Education offered a three-year course in education, psychology, sociology etc., and specialisation in one practical subject. (Standards were high and among the first batch of students, failure rates for different areas of specialisation were from thirty to sixty per cent.) The Institute held promise of feeding committed and competent instructors to the Village Institutes, which initially drew heavily on the staff of the urban teacher training schools – staff presumably somewhat ill-prepared to develop the message of the Village Institutes to the full. (The ordinary teacher training schools were allowed to run down during the 1940s but resumed their former scale of operations in the 1950s when the Village Institutes were suppressed. Many Village Institute staff were then transferred to posts in the ordinary training schools.)

Recruitment by the Village Institutes in 1940-1 was 2,490 (including 235 girls) and a peak intake of 3,750 was reached in 1943. The number of diplomas awarded each year ranged from a minimum of 1,700 to a maximum of 2,269. The total number of diplomas awarded prior to the closure of the institutes was 17,162. This figure may be compared with the approximate number of villages in the country, some 40,000. A fair beginning had been made in training teachers for the village schools and the discontinuation of the Village Institute programme before the full needs of the rural population had been met seems unfortunate. It is not clear, however, what proportion of teachers trained subsequently in the ordinary teacher training colleges came from a rural background. Presumably more did than in the 1930s and they may have been willing to accept rural appointments despite their more orthodox training. The problem of staffing the rural schools remained, however, since as late as 1964 there were over one and a half million children living in villages where there were no schools.

It may be noted here that graduates of the Village Institutes were obliged to serve as village teachers for twenty years or else to repay to the government the full or partial costs of their training – unless they were nominated for higher training. Graduates unable or unwilling to take up teaching were, however, permitted to practise certain rural crafts specified by the Ministry of Education.

Regarding the outcomes of the programme at school level, there is little data available in English. Village Institute graduates had their apologists, for example Tongua's son, who claimed that they had worked vigorously toward social reform. Their critics in contrast, claimed that the Village Institute course was overloaded, that the graduates were unable to prepare students for secondary school entrance, that they were disaffected with the existing social order and lacked influence with the conservative peasantry who respected age and experience and religious orthodoxy.

Review of Strategy

The strategy underlying the foundation of the Village Institutes represented a forceful combination of the normative re-educative strategy and the use of the government's legal powers. Rural youth were to be offered a programme of training aligned to Atatürk's programme for rural uplift, a training long enough for them to develop new loyalties and long enough also for them to acquire a good grounding in practical studies. They were further to be compelled by law to undertake the duties for which they had been trained – and social circumstances evidently permitted this sanction to be enforced. (There may also have been limited scope for Village Institute graduates in the towns.) The authorities, in turn, were compelled by law to supply the necessary conditions for community education.

The nature of the educational innovation was likewise broadly defined by law but teachers were left free to interpret these instructions in the light of local circumstances (and had a training which conferred a basic competence such that the able and diligent student could do so). The Village Institutes themselves, as an innovation system, had their strengths and weaknesses. Their strength was an attention to detail. Their weakness was the need to accomplish so much with students who were relatively immature.

Initially, the programme accorded in a way with villagers' professed interests. Villagers were reported in the 1920s as seeing no point in schooling which lacked relevance to village life. It was claimed, however, that villagers became discontented because Village Institute graduates lacked the attainments in academic subjects required to prepare children for secondary school entrance. How far the villagers welcomed the agricultural and technical expertise brought to them by the Village Institute graduates is uncertain. The fact that the Village Institute programme discounted religion whereas the villagers valued religious instruction for their children would have generated a conflict between the values of teachers (and of the government which sent them) and the values of the peasantry, acting counter to the objective of communicating new skills and new ways of thinking.

Teacher motivation was on the whole well provided for. The long period of study at the Village Institutes would have tended to generate a sense of identity with the reformers' modernisation philosophy. Every effort was made to confer the competence required of the prospective teachers – often to be youthful founder-principals of the schools where they were to work. The system of bonded service provided reinforcement of the sense of commitment should it weaken. And the post of rural schoolteacher with a government salary to be supplemented by the teacher's own 'model' farming, may have been welcome to rural youth for whom few other openings were available.

The presumed attachment of Village Institute graduates to Atatürk's reformist, anti-religious philisophy again (as with the Mexican venture) prevented the concept of 'relevance' from becoming a natural educational technicality, however. It was a prime cause of the suppression of the institutes when the conservative Menderes government came to power in 1950. Even the coalition government of the late 1940s had modified the curriculum. The study of controversial subjects such as psychology and sociology was abolished, and the ministers who had initiated the institute programme were dismissed. In the early 1950s, Islamic education was added to the timetable. These changes were deemed insufficient, however. The institutes had encouraged their students to internalise ideals such 'modernisation' and 'progress' and to abjure religion, tradition and a feudal social order. Hence the very institutes themselves could not long be tolerated when the electorate voted for an end to Atatürk's politics. The institutes had to be closed, even though the staff were in large measure transferred to the orthodox teacher training colleges, which were revived at this time.

How far the closure measures represented a change of name and how far there was a major change in emphasis and policy as regards 'relevance' topics is not easy to judge. It is clear, however, that the dynamic which had been built up in favour of ruralised teacher training was lost. Those who had argued for closure of the institutes and for a unified educational structure at all levels as the basis for national integration prevailed. It would have been all too easy for any residual impulse towards training in agriculture, craftwork etc. to lose its force, and for practical subjects to become the Cinderellas they so often are in relation to academic studies. A carefully designed, locally adapted, gradualist venture had come to an end. As in Mexico, the attempt to convey a reformist philosophy alongside practical studies in agriculture, crafts and health led ultimately to the discontinuation of the programme. Interestingly, the same weakness may be attributed to Gandhian Basic Education, an account of which now follows.

Gandhian Basic Education in India

Gandhian Basic Education provides an interesting contrast to the initiatives in Mexico and Turkey. It developed quite strongly in the late 1940s and the 1950s yet it came to a definite halt in the 1960s. This termination was *not* associated with any abrupt change in political policies, however. Congress remained in power and due respect continued to be paid to Gandhi and his educational thinking, while Basic Education, as he conceived it, was discontinued as the basis of national policy.

This case study is also distinguished by the volume of documentation available, including an official evaluation report published in 1956 which listed implementation problems and weaknesses. If the problems encountered in the Gandhian venture are given emphasis it is because of the coherent published materials available. There is no reason to suppose that programmes in other countries encountered or encounter less problems or have been significantly better administered. Rather, the reverse may be the case. An administration sufficiently committed to initiate and publicise an evaluation study may well reflect commitment and competence on the part of many who have been directly involved in programme implementation.

Origin

Two streams converged to generate the programme of Basic National Education. One was the National Education Movement, founded by Gokhale, Lala Lajpat Rai and others, which sought Indian control of the education system and inculcation of respect for Indian languages, traditions and culture. This movement was fired by the public indignation over Lord Curzon's partition of Bengal in 1904, and in the decade that followed, over fifty 'national' high schools were set up in that province. The movement had subsided by 1920 but was revived by Gandhi's call for students to withdraw from government-sponsored schools and colleges, as part of the non-co-operation programme in 1920-2. Over a thousand 'national' schools and colleges were set up in connection with the non-co-operation movement, but only a few of these institutions continued permanently. As it became evident that the struggle for independence would last for some time, the idea of setting up national institutions in parallel with the official system was given up, with the idea that once self-government was attained, national education would be provided on a universal basis by the state.[5]

Basic National Education, the 'Wardha scheme', took its special character from the life and experiences of Gandhi. He often referred in later years to his experience of teaching the twenty or thirty children, including his own sons, who were resident on the agricultural commune near Johannesburg, known as Tolstoy Farm (Gandhi 1927, Fischer 1951). This personal experience of the education of the young convinced Gandhi of the central role which productive work could and should play in the educational process.

For many years after his return to India in 1915, Gandhi was only intermittently and tangentially concerned with education. His intimate acquaintance with rural life and experience in the development of rural crafts during this period nevertheless contributed much to his formulation in 1937 of a system of Basic Education centred around the life and work of a rehabilitated rural community. During this period, Gandhi identified spinning as a craft which could be feasibly introduced into every classroom and which could provide a means of subsistence to those who wished to continue with it after leaving school.[6]

A reservoir of low-cost technology and of skills in this particular craft was already available when the Basic Education programme was launched in 1937-8. Following the election of Congress ministries in several states, Gandhi published a series of articles in his journal *Harijan*, in which his ideas for educational reform were spelled out. For example,

> 1. Primary education, extending over a period of seven years or longer, and covering all the subjects up to matriculation standard, except English, plus a vocation used as the vehicle for drawing out the minds of boys and girls in all departments of knowledge, should take the place of what passes today under the name of primary, middle and high school education.
> 2. Such education taken as a whole, can, and must be self-supporting; in fact, self-support is the acid test of its reality.[7]

The acid test because 'the child at the age of 14, that is after finishing a seven years' course, should be discharged as an earning unit . . . . You impart education and simultaneously cut at the root of unemployment.'[8]

Overt Objectives

Basic Education was explicitly concerned with the development of professional competence in craft areas such as spinning, so that school-leavers were competent to earn a living using these skills. It was equally concerned with the diffusion throughout Indian society of more positive attitudes to manual work, traditionally despised by the upper castes. It was again vitally concerned with craftwork as a means of off-setting the cost of schooling – Gandhi saw this as a means of bringing universal and relevant primary education to the villages despite the acute budgetary constraints of the times. He believed further that his objective of covering the existing high school curriculum, less English, could be better accomplished when pursued simultaneously with craft training, since education correlated with concrete activities would be more meaningful to children than the endless reproduction of notes. Gandhi stressed also the detrimental effect on health of a heavy load of bookish schooling, hoping that through handicraft and agricultural work, Basic school pupils would retain their natural strength and vigour. In the 1940s he stressed also the need to view Basic Education as a lifelong process and urged Basic Educators to provide for the needs of the adult population.

In addition he stressed the intrinsic rewards of craftwork. It was perhaps his own experience of these intrinsic rewards that led him to formulate his objectives in visionary terms.

> This education is meant to transform children into model villagers . . . Basic education links the children . . . to all that is best and lasting in India. It develops both the body and the mind, and keeps the child rooted to the soil with a glorious vision of the future in the realisation of which he or she begins to take his or her share from the very commencement of his or her career in school.[9]

At the same time he sought wider societal changes which would complement Basic Education in leading towards the uplift and transformation of rural life.

It may be asked whether Gandhi sought specifically to restrict the Basic school graduate to his village, but this is inconsistent with his philosophy. There is no evidence that he intended able children from Basic schools to be at a disadvantage, in orthodox terms, in relation to children attending non-Basic schools. In that he was concerned with the design of a new kind of education for a new kind of society, he expected all educational insitutions to be transformed and all children to follow the Basic programme once independence was won and the new society founded.[10] Under these circumstances there would have been no question of Basic-educated children being at a disadvantage in gaining admission to higher studies or modern-sector employment. He knew as well as any that parents pressed their sons to gain a middle school, matriculation or college certificate, in order to try for a modern-sector job. He no doubt hoped that Basic Education would lessen this pressure. But he surely had no intention of putting Basic school graduates at a disadvantage pending reorganisation of the education system as a whole. Indeed, he noted that a Basic school graduate, should he go on to college, would probably do better than the other students, on account of the greater pertinence of his education. The version of Basic Education developed by the governmental Central Advisory Board of Education did in principle provide for the transfer of academically talented pupils from Basic schools to high school. The recommendations of two subcommittees chaired by B.G. Kher (Premier and Education Minister, Bombay) in 1938-9, incorporated in the Board's Report on Post-War Educational Development in India, provided for

Junior Basic Edcuation from age 6 to 11 and Senior Basic Education from age 11 to 14 (eight years in all), with transfer of able pupils to the proposed six-year high schools from both Junior Basic (at 11+) and Senior Basic institutions.[11] These recommendations for transfer machinery were not systematically taken up, however.

Development and Outcomes

Gandhi's scheme for educational reform, endorsed by a Conference at Wardha in 1937, and adopted by the Indian National Congress in March 1938, was launched after a report by the Zakir Husain Committee, which led to the first institution of Basic Education – the Vidya Mandir Training School, in Wardha later the same year.[12]

Experimental Basic schools were opened by the Congress governments in the various states and by several private institutions such as the Jamia Millia Islamia in Delhi and the Gujarat Vidyapeeth. Unfortunately, the Congress governments resigned shortly thereafter, in early 1940, and many of the experimental schools started by them were closed or continued 'in a state of suspended animation'.[13] In Bihar the experiment continued, however, and a government report on the work of the 27 Basic schools in Champaran district during 1940-1, commented favourably on their progress.

The post-war years saw a revival of Basic Education programmes as Gandhian workers were released from detention, but constitutional and inter-communal problems limited the attention which Gandhi and the Congress could give to educational matters. Shortly after independence, Gandhi was dead. To the loss of impetus caused by the war was added the absence of leadership, since there was no one else of national stature to respond both creatively and authoritatively to the challenges of large-scale implementation. Instead there came conflicting interpretations of his message and, increasingly, an unwillingness to accept the policy of universal Basic Education.

One state – Uttar Pradesh – went ahead and introduced the Basic approach in all its primary schools from July 1948. Uttar Pradesh had earlier devoted considerable resources to in-service training programmes for teachers and on this basis felt able to proceed. A second factor contributing to the policy of immediate conversion was the interpretation placed upon Basic Education by this state. Craftwork was seen predominantly as a creative activity, and the value of pupils' output was treated as secondary. Given this change of emphasis it was possible to go ahead quickly even though funds for purchasing the full range of craft equipment might not be available for some time. The problem of a dualistic system of primary education was avoided but at the expense of some schools being called Basic when little had changed except their name.

Elsewhere in India the strategy of gradualism was adopted, with substantial inter-state variation. The number of Junior Basic schools, outside Uttar Pradesh, rose from 1,400 in 1950-1 to 11,073 in 1955-6, and to 30,908 in 1963-4. The number of Senior Basic schools rose from 388 in 1950-1 to 4,842 in 1955-6 and to 17,036 by 1963-4 (all-India totals). At the same time, however, there had been a continuing growth in the number of non-Basic schools. Between 1950-1 and 1963-4 over 117,000 non-Basic primary schools and over 35,000 non-Basic middle schools were constructed. The net addition to the stock of non-Basic schools outnumbered the total number of Basic schools created both by construction of new schools and conversion to existing ones. This distortion of government policy was due in part to the pressure of public demand for non-Basic schools and in part to the lesser cost of ordinary schools.[14]

The Demise of Basic Education

The problems confronted by Basic Education finally led to an erosion of governmental and popular support for the programme. The first Five Year Plan gave considerable space to a discussion of Basic Education and the strategies to be adopted to ensure its successful implementation. Even the third Five Year Plan, published in 1962, provided for the conversion of about 57,760 schools to the Basic model, for the conversion of all unconverted training schools to the Basic approach, and for a link-up between Basic Education and local development activities. Yet the *Fourth Five Year Plan: a Draft Outline,* published in 1966, made no mention of Basic Education at all. On elementary education it merely stated that the emphasis would be on 'free and universal primary education, elimination of wastage, and work orientation of the curriculum'.

This change of policy would seem to reflect, not only the impact of implementation problems (discussed later) but also the widespread support for the idea that India should move forward through the application of modern science and technology to development problems (a topic arousing international interest in the 1960s) with an emphasis on industrialisation and 'modernised' agriculture. This idea was a focal point in the thinking of the Education Commission of 1964-6, a panel of distinguished Indian and foreign educationists who adopted an avowedly modernist approach to development problems.

The Gandhian strategy of education for rural reconstruction through intermediate or appropriate technology was largely neglected. In place of the Basic concept, the commission put forward a four-fold curriculum based on:

- 'literacy' or a study of languages, humanities and social sciences
- 'numeracy' or a study of mathematics and natural sciences
- work experience
- social service.[15]

The latter two elements represented the legacy of Gandhi's attempt to make education directly relevant to the life and work of the community.[16]

Perhaps to avoid controversy, the Education Commission omitted any analysis of the Basic Education venture or of the lessons that could be learned from it in developing the proposed programmes of work experience and social service. The commission's recommendations were largely accepted by the central and state governments and from 1966 the commission's formula, and work experience, represented official educational policy and Basic education was left to find its own way. In many states it faded from prominence, though some individual Basic Education centres remained strong. In Gujarat, Gandhi's home state, a continuing programme for the construction of residential post-Basic high schools in the backward areas has brought the total of such schools to over one hundred.

Review of Strategy

The strategy suggested in the Zakir Husain report was based on government action – gradualist but with a strong forward impetus. The normative re-educative approach was given considerable weight, through emphasis on teacher training. One or more 'compact areas' in each state were to be selected for the immediate introduction of Basic Education. A three-year Basic teacher training school was to be established immediately in each such district and 'the work of establishing basic schools for all the children in the selected area should be completed within five years'. At the same time, all existing teacher training schools were to be converted to the Basic model. Condensed one-year courses of training in the Basic approach were to be introduced for experienced teachers, to supplement the preferably three-year pre-service courses. All elementary-school teachers were to attend brief introductory courses in Basic education with the space of five years. As more teachers emerged from the Basic training colleges in each state, 'new basic schools should be started in a selected area where as far as possible all the schools should be of the new type contemplated. It does not seem desirable that schools of the present as well as the new type should co-exist in the same area. Naturally it will be easier and more useful to select for this purpose areas in which there are few schools at present and where, for that reason, the provision of educational facilities is more urgently required.'[17] (The possible difficulties of coexistence between the new and old types of schooling were noted here. But the 'compact area' method suggested by the Zakir Husain Committee as a means of avoiding these difficulties was later thought to have been a brake upon progress.) The need for organisations at state and national level to prepare new textbooks, guidelines for the teachers etc., was also recognised by the Zakir Husain Committee.

The policy of gradualism has much to commend it, but it can become the pretext for bureaucratic inertia. The Assessment Commitee on Basic Education took the view in 1956 that the strategy of gradual development in 'compact areas' had degenerated into stagnation. The committee recommended that all schools should be adapted forthwith to incorporate the general principles of Basic Education (a recommendation sufficiently general to be universally accepted) and that the transformation of all schools to the Basic model proper incorporating a full complement of craftwork should be completed gradually but within a period of five to seven years (a recommendation universally ignored). It recommended administrative changes in the State Departments of Education to give effect to this strategy, suggesting that administrative weaknesses and indifference had been at the root of earlier failures.

The Basic Education experience shows essentially the dangers of a weakly administered 'coercive' or 'political-administrative' approach, whether a policy of immediate system-wide reform or a policy of gradualism is adopted. After Gandhi's death, the impetus behind the idea of Basic Education was lost, and although Basic Education was adopted as the target for educational development, too many key people had private reservations about it for the necessary push to be made. The diffusion of responsibility in a federal system, where schooling was the responsibility of the states but received some support from federal funds, did not help. The role of the central government in respect of Basic Education was indirect (except in the Union Territories for which it was responsible): exhortation and advice, together with a subsidy of 50 per cent for expenditure on the Basic Education programmes included in the successive five-year development plans. The all-India Hindustani Talimi Sangh likewise lacked authority to intervene. It was thus possible for administrators in the states to argue that the official policy for the system-wide introduction of Basic Education was unrealistic in view of the state's budgetary constraints, while at the centre there was no substantial and influential body of persons working full time on the resolution of implementation problems.

A major problem regarding the type of innovation was the substantial capital investment required to implement the craft-centred programme. The full list of equipment for spinning (grades 1 to 5) and weaving (grades 6 and 7) in a Basic school would have cost about Rs.60 if only one item of each type was bought, but the equipment specified for a school of seven grades with 30 students in each was estimated by them to cost Rs.1,000 or more while another Rs.500 would be required for working capital (stocks of cotton etc.), in addition to substantial expenditure on agricultural equipment, land, cardboard, woodwork and metalwork equipment.

While it would have been possible to do spinning and weaving cheaply using hand spindles and simple frame looms, this was not the kind of programme envisaged by the Husain Committee (though Gandhi talked of relying on hand spindles). The pupil was expected to gain as full an understanding of the various technologies of spinning and weaving as any Gandhian worker. Thus the Grade 5 curriculum, for instance, includes the use of the Yeravda *charka*, the Magan *charka* and the Savli *charka*, up to prescribed standards of efficiency. And the purchase of 20 looms was prescribed for use by pupils of grades 6 and 7.

The Quinquennial Education Review for 1947-52 noted that 'deficiency of equipment appeared to be chronic over the period under review and this hampered productive work'.

The Assessment Committee noted the same problems in 1956. Apart from the pròblem that many converted schools were still located in the old overcrowded school buildings, making practical work very difficult, they stressed the frequent and less excusable absence of a minimal supply of craft materials and equipment.

A survey of teacher training schools in Gujarat conducted in 1965 revealed that even here the provision of land, buildings and equipment for craftwork was insufficient. And this was in a state where cotton grows in every other field and is administered from the textile centre of Ahmedabad. From Maharashtra, another state which should have been able to do better, came similar reports (Merra 1970:56).

Insofar as craftwork in Basic schools was not subject to external examinations, there was, in principle, full scope for schools to adopt a wide range of activities based upon local resources and the circumstances of the school. However, a number of educators have commented on the narrow interpretation given to craftwork – typically gardening and the spinning of cotton. Cotton-spinning was often taken up even in areas where raw cotton was not readily available and where alternative local resources could have been utilised in the programme. This rigidity may be attributed in part to the emphasis given from the time of the Zakir Husain report to textile work and agriculture (together with woodwork and metalwork) as crafts permitting extensive correlation with ordinary school subjects. The principle of achieving professional standards in one major and one subsidiary craft also worked against flexibility which might have permitted several locally appropriate crafts to be introduced on a supplementary or experimental basis. Perhaps the most restricting factor, however, was the mental or emotional equation of Gandhi with spinning.

The fact is, however, that it is very difficult to conceive of productive activities that can readily be organised on a mass scale and relate to real market opportunities, and that it was difficult for the average administrator to improve Gandhi's choice of spinning (feasible even in overcrowded classrooms and with a wide range of technical options including the very cheap hand spindle) and agriculture.

As regards the induction system for teachers and other educators, and the provision for supportive research and development, these were inadequate to the concept of Basic Education put forward by Gandhi. A substantial effort was indeed made to transform pre-service teacher training to the Basic model. Thus in 1950-1, some 15 per cent of all training schools were Basic (114 in all, the Uttar Pradesh colleges still not having been converted) while in 1955-6 some 56 per cent were Basic (520, including 97 in Uttar Pradesh).[18] The 423 Basic training schools outside Uttar Pradesh at the latter date may be compared with the approximately 16,000 Basic schools outside Uttar Pradesh in the same year. These figures are not too disproportionate, if it could be assumed that most graduates of the training insitutions went to Basic schools. Since, however, some states had adopted a process of introducing Basic-oriented curricula in all the schools (this became national and state policy everywhere in the late 1950s) there would have been some tendency for the Basic-trained teachers to opt for employment in Basic-oriented schools nearer to the large cities rather than in fully Basic rural schools in more isolated regions.

Provision for in-service training of teachers varied from state to state. Both pre-service and in-service training suffered, however, from the relative neglect of research and development work. Despite their training, teachers often failed to understand what exactly was intended. From the Zakir Husain report on, there would seem to have been some confusion as to how attention should be divided between the fairly orthodox list of subjects spelled out in the main body of the report, and the 'centres of correlation'. Originally Gandhi had proposed that *all* teaching should be related to craftwork as a centre of correlation. This idea is relatively straightforward and an annex to the Zakir Husain report showed that a very full primary school curriculum covering language, arithmetic, social studies, science etc. could be developed around spinning and weaving as the centre of correlation. The educationists advising Gandhi convinced him, however, that there should be two further centres of correlation – the natural environment and the social environment. Hence the school principal or teacher who studied the Zakir Husain report and annexes might find three different approaches spelled out:

- craftwork as the centre of correlation for teaching each subject area
- craftwork plus the natural and social environments of the locality as the centre of correlation for teaching each subject area
- a 'relevant' but orthodox looking syllabus to be 'covered' for each subject area, including craftwork as a subject area in its own right.

It was also unclear how much of the correlated teaching should be given while practical work was in progress and how much was to feature in the 'classwork' allocation on the timetable.

It had been recognised early on that a great deal of experimental work would be needed and that teachers' handbooks etc. would be required. But, partly from controversies and inertia, progress in this respect was very slow, and teachers had to operate without adequate guidelines and support. The authors of the Five Year Plan progress report for 1953-4 pointed out the seriousness of the situation, but the problem of inadequate professional support continued to the end. Induction of supervisory staff had also been weak, and perhaps they also were discouraged by a lack of clarity regarding the nature of the Basic innovation.

A fundamental weakness of the Basic school system was lack of client motivation. The Zakir Husain Committee did not envisage a long-term dualism within the education system – they had envisaged the speedy transformation of the education system as a whole along the lines proposed by Gandhi. Interim arrangements were, however, specifically considered by the Central Advisory Board of Education, but its recommendations were largely ignored. The slow progress towards Basic Education in most states thus undermined support for Gandhi's educational legacy. Instead there developed a general antipathy towards Basic schooling, since graduates from Basic schools had for some years no clear rights of access to high school classes preparing for the matriculation examination – the key to higher education or middle level employment and to upward social mobility for rural children.

Weaknesses in the system for transfer of Basic pupils to the matriculation stream meant that the decisions for or against acceptance often lay in the hands of headmasters and administrators who held a poor view of Basic schooling. Chettiar conducted a survey which showed that the public in general and high school principals in particular believed that academic standards were lower in Basic schools. Reasons advanced for this belief included: 'absence of textbooks; time is taken up by other activities; the method of correlation is difficult; sufficient number of guide books are not available; practice in the 3 Rs is less; memorisation is reduced; there is no sequence in learning; basic education is not suited for homework'. Chettiar commented wryly: 'The public expect the school to give a formal academic type of education. They judge the school by the amount of bookish homework given and by the pupils' carrying textbooks to and from the school.'[19]

The Assessment Committee noted in 1956 that no state had made unambiguous plans for giving post-Basic (secondary) schooling a place alongside high schools and multi-purpose schools in respect of access to higher education. Chettiar made the same point in 1964.

In contrast, the subsequent provision in the State of Gujarat for post-Basic (high) school pupils to sit the State matriculation examination, taking specially provided elective subjects, and the provision for Basic courses at teacher training, first degree and post-graduate level, have ensured the survival of Basic Education as a real, if small-scale, alternative to the orthodox system. Even in Gujarat, however, Basic Education has mainly been a matter for backward rural communities. The more influential city dwellers and the well-to-do prefer the orthodox curricula which they feel will give their children a better chance of doing well in matriculation and college examinations and a better training in English. Gandhi was against the teaching of English, which in his time was crucial to the elite as the vehicle for teaching in the upper high school classes and at college, and was required for senior government appointments. (Many Basic schools did in fact offer English as an extra subject, in response to popular demand.)

The motivation of teachers was often weak, caught as they were between unenthusiastic supervisors and unenthusiastic parents. Lack of necessary resources and inadequate training served to discourage them further. A report from a not atypical state (Mysore) offered the following picture:

> In most places, village teachers were opposed to the Basic ideology . . . From the experience of the last five years, a teacher in a Basic school needs all his energy, time and intelligence to convince the villager of the advantages of Basic education. The present grades, allowances and living conditions of Basic teachers are not sufficiently attractive to induce people to work wholeheartedly for this type of education.

The report of the Assessment Committee on Basic Education confirmed the general picture.

It is clear that Basic Education was one of the most exciting ventures in relevant education. Unfortunately the implementation phase followed Gandhi's death, for it seems likely that, had he lived, a more workable strategy might have been evolved.

The Education Commission's decision in 1966 to drop the term 'Basic' while retaining the concepts of work experience and social service as curriculum adjuncts represented a belated response to two decades of trial and error. It may be argued, however, that had the composition of the commission been different, or the climate of thought more favourable to the Gandhian philosophy in general (as it was again in 1977), then the new proposals might have been presented as a restructuring of Basic Education rather than a replacement for it. However, the tardy and lukewarm response to the commission's proposals for work-experience programmes indicates that the same factors which held back Basic Education have been at work since. Widespread diffusion of decision-making power, widespread lack of conviction regarding the work-experience concept, and lack of material resources, have combined with lack of client and teacher motivation to constrain development.

The Philippines Community Schools

Origin and Overt Objectives[20]

The Philippines has had a tradition of including some kind of work skills, study of hygiene and so on in the school curriculum dating back to the early 1900s. It reflects in part the influence of the 'industrial education' movement in the USA. Close links with the USA ensured also that leading Philippine educators were acquainted with the inter-war community school movement there. Dr Pedro Orata, for example, had run a community school to serve the needs of an American Indian community. The aftermath of war left the Philippines of the late 1940s in a state of turmoil, and several of these educators felt that the community school approach could help to revive the nation. They began experimental schools; Orata in his home province of Pangasinan, Dr Aquilar in Iliolo, Superintendent Gaffud in Cagayan. Their approaches and objectives varied but the movement gained ground, especially after the restructured Philippines Association of School Superintendents was set up in 1949. The Association initiated a ten-year programme for improving education in rural areas. The topics selected for their annual conventions indicate the nature of their concerns:

1949 Education for community living.
1950 Education in rural areas for better living.
1951 Adult education.
1952 Gearing the curriculum to rural living.
1953 Improving the community school programme for economic development.
1954 Vitalising the community school for moral and civic education in a democracy.
1955 Evaluating the community school programme during the last 5 years.

The objectives of the community school movement were later summarised as: making the school a centre for the education of adults in life skills and democracy; enriching education through the use of community resources and through a curriculum core built around human living; improvement of the community through pupils studying and participating in its problems; improvement through joint school community projects.

Programme development

The Bureau of Public Schools endorsed the idea of community schools and circulated particulars of the various approaches that had been developed: 'direct labour' by pupils in community service projects; 'indirect approach' to community uplift through relevant classroom teaching; 'dual approach' – education of children and adults separately; 'unitary approach' where some studies were undertaken by children and adults together; 'Laguna approach', where children as members of 'junior *puroks*' (the *purok* was a traditional neighbourhood group, revitalised in a democratic form by some community school leaders) visited community *puroks* and held discussion classes there each week.

The bureau did not directly finance community school activities, but met local expenditures in setting up, jointly with UNESCO, the Philippines Community School Training Centre, opened in 1953 at Bayambang in Pangasinan province.

The early 1950s also saw community development work by other agencies, and in 1956 the Office of the Presidential Assistant on Community Development was established to coordinate community work. In response to this movement towards rationalisation and to a general feeling that children had spent too much of their schooltime on community work, the schools were encouraged to concentrate mainly on the 'indirect approach' whereby classroom studies would lead to community uplift through better understanding of the principles of health, agriculture, community organisation etc. Schools were permitted to continue with project work if they so wished, however.

In the early 1950s many concrete manifestations of the programme, in terms of ventures relating to health and sanitation, agriculture and animal husbandry, village beautification, literacy classes and community reading centres were established. By the mid 1950s, however, educators joined parents in acknowledging that the time spent on community service had been to the detriment of the study of the three Rs and other subjects. In a very frank address to school and training college supervisors in the Philippines in 1956, the Director of Public Schools himself called attention to the fact that 'in our effort to implement the community education programme on the basis of the way in which we have interpreted it, we have wittingly or unwittingly done violence to accepted educational values and standards'. He did not condemn the idea of community schools, but he suggested a different approach was needed (Batten 1959: 154-5).

Review of Strategy

District superintendents initiated the community school movement, some beginning with pilot schools, others asking all schools to introduce community-related activities. The government's role was one of approving the decentralised initiatives and encouraging all schools to participate. No particular formula was laid down, nor was there any formal assessment of pupils' activities.

Schools were left free to develop their own approach to the design of the community school programme and numerous different activities were attempted, as indicated earlier. Regarding innovation systems designed to introduce educators to the community school concept, there is little documentation for the early years. The Community School Training Centre, set up with UNESCO assistance in 1953, was intended to strengthen the induction and research and development functions.

U.H. Fleege, head of the UNESCO mission to the training centre, noted that teachers lacked the technical and organisational skills to undertake the projects required of them, lacked a rural background, and had difficulty in integrating community studies with orthodox classroom teaching. He noted also inadequate understanding of the community school concept and inadequate leadership on the part of educational administrators.[21]

Certainly a weak point in the programme was the responsiveness of the schools' clients to the community schools innovation. Many parents objected to their pupils being diverted from academic studies which could lead on to high school studies or at least a better chance of a paid job of some kind. The poor saw little value in the 'economic' projects, lacking the funds to take advantage of new skills acquired, and disliked their children spoiling their school clothes with street cleaning and catching pigs. The slightly more affluent objected to children undertaking low-status activities. Teachers were left to carry pupils and parents with them by their own powers of persuasion. They often met apathy, even resistance, but were sometimes successful.[22]

A typical response concerned a school project to transform a swamp into fishponds. Parents complained: 'Digging is a man's job. Spare the children from the forced labour that the project will require. They ought not to spoil their clothes by being forced to work in muddy places. Besides, why should they waste their precious study time that is not even enough to enable them to learn to read and write?'[23]

Teacher motivation was likewise patchy. Many teachers were unable to cope with the range of activities required by school or district policy. The supervisory staff again emerge as a key factor here. Batten (1959: 125-6) commented on the load confronting a teacher who had to undertake a great deal of work with adults as well as children, especially if the teacher had 'the misfortune to work under an ambitious and dictatorial supervisor'.

The Philippines community school movement is an interesting example of an initiative which began on a decentralised basis and gained government support on 'rational-empirical' grounds. It appears to have been a natural response to the conditions of the time. The attempt to universalise the programme, as a means of ameliorating urgent social and economic problems was, however, counter-productive. Naive interpretations of the sophisticated community school concept generated negative reactions from the schools' clients as well as teachers. Had the coverage been less extensive, and worked from teacher idealism, innovativeness and competence as the basic driving force, quality might have been more favourable. The community orientation has in fact continued in certain schools and the barrio high school movement launched in the 1960s incorporated similar features to be adopted on a voluntary basis. Orata's account of the barrio high school movement, giving examples of its successes, illustrates well the potential for building a network of 'relevance' ventures on a voluntary principle where circumstances are favourable (Orata 1969, 1972).

A footnote: the 1972 Presidential Commission on education failed to mention community schools in its report. Its later explanation was that in the Philippines all schools are community schools.

The 1950s Tanganyika Agricultural Programme

Origins and Overt Objectives[24]

Western education came to Tanzania in the late nineteenth century through Christian missionaries. Subsequently the German colonial administration set up state schools. The colonial authorities recruited school-leavers to occupy minor administrative posts and, hence, by the 1920s the concept that schooling led on to salaried employment was well established. The continued expansion of schooling by the missions led to official apprehension. The first British Director of Education was 'obsessed with the bogey of educational overproduction' and took the view that 'The ideal for a system of African education would be that based on an employment census and a careful forecast of economic development.' He believed that a census of African children would reveal that 'the vast majority look upon school as a means to become a clerk or a teacher or to enter other sedentary employment'. Hence the government's determination that if education was to expand it must be linked to agriculture, as indicated in the following statement to the Legislative Council:

> In any vision of future development agriculture must occupy the foremost place . . . Everything, therefore, points to agriculture as the basis of our educational system in the elementary stages.

This exhortation, reflecting the contemporary British preoccupation with 'adapted' education, did not lead to very impressive results. The missions were happy to include agriculture on the school timetable, as it fitted in theory with their desire to build up self-contained, prosperous, rural communities of Christian converts. On the pedagogical side they were often weak, however. Cameron and Dodd (1970) comment that agricultural education of some kind or another was imparted in all schools at all levels but 'as often as not it degenerated into mere manual labour on large, non-typical holdings to supplement fee revenue'. The inadequacy of agricultural instruction in schools and teacher training institutions was likewise a regular theme in the annual reports of the Director of Education. There was no pressure from African parents to remedy these weaknesses – they pressed rather for a greater emphasis on academic subjects, aware that children who reached the sixth grade of primary school were virtually certain of a paid job (Morrison 1976:59).

In 1948 a new Director of Education, encouraged by the enthusiasm of an important chief, revived the idea of a practical bias in the schools. By then, the number of pupils completing primary school had increased and not all could obtain the type of employment previously available.

A new system of schooling was therefore introduced in 1950, comprising three four-year cycles of education – primary, middle school and secondary. This circumstance led to an explicit attempt at formulating the objectives of the new 'middle' school:

> The middle school course is designed to be complete in itself so that those who pass through it, whether they proceed further or not, will have received an education which will assist them to follow in more intelligent and capable manner whatever pursuits they take up and, generally, to play a more useful part in the development of the locality to which they belong. To this end the form and bias of the course at any particular school will, so far as possible, be related to the needs and reflect the life of the area in which the school is situated. In an agricultural area, for example, the bias will be agricultural, in a pastoral area the bias will be more towards animal husbandry, while in an urban area the bias may be commercial or industrial. In the girls' middle schools there will also be, in all cases, a bias towards homecraft. These biases will be of a practical nature and will form a special feature of the middle school course. (Cited in Dodd 1969:6.)

The statement of objectives carefully avoided a commitment to teaching specific vocationally useful skills. 'The course would aim not so much at training young people to be fully equipped farmers but would rather instil in them the proper orientation toward their future roles as farmers', notes Dodd (1969) in a discussion of course objectives. The desirability of correlating practical activities and classroom studies to the benefit of both was also stressed.

There was also emphasis on the objective of character development which again featured strongly in the summary of the objectives of the middle school programme as a whole by the authors of the 1952 *Provisional Syllabus of Instruction for Middle Schools.* Here again the objective of character development seems to have been linked in the authors' minds with the experience of undertaking agricultural and other projects.

The parallel in objectives between these 1950s school programmes and the later initiative in 'education for self-reliance' is striking, as has been noted by Dodd (1969), and illustrates the way in which the objectives cited for a programme reflect a country's current economic and social circumstances. The objective of conveying useful skills to backward communities was not stressed in either case because of the existence of professional extension services for this purpose, and likewise the objective of teaching new skills to the pupils was played down, since they too would have access to such services on leaving school. An important difference between the British scheme and that of President Nyerere is that the British scheme was conceived in a paternalistic context. Nyerere's proposals are clearly intended to benefit his people (but are vulnerable in the implementation phases) whereas the 1950s programme could be perceived as a control imposed upon Africans (Asian and European schools were exempt) by a colonial government anxious to raise the productivity and stability of a subservient agricultural labour force, a political constraint which ultimately helped to seal its fate in conjunction with other social, economic and educational forces. (See Dodd 1969.)

Programme Development

A special feature of the new agricultural programmes was the provision of a detailed syllabus for classroom and practical work. Classroom studies were spelled out for each grade, covering topics such as seeds, the growth of plants etc. in the primary school and with more advanced agricultural topics incorporated in the general science curriculum of the middle school. Practical work was to include a variety of activities but especial emphasis was to be given to the idea of experimental plots. Primary school lessons were to be related to work on fifteen ¼-acre demonstration plots (roughly half of these fallow), designed to illustrate tie-ridging, use of manure, rotation, alternative crops etc. Variations in cropping plans were suggested for different regions. The middle school syllabus specified a programme requiring sixteen plots of $^1/_{16}$-acre together with a 20-acre 'production farm' (4 acres cultivated, 4 acres fallow, 12 acres grazing) and provision for animal husbandry. The farm was to be operated by grade 9 pupils, while the experimental plots were to be tended by pupils in grades 5 to 7. Each grade was to undertake selected experiments, e.g. spacing, seed selection, timely planting and catch-cropping in grade 5.

The Fuggles-Couchman report of 1956 revealed the limited progress that had been made in developing these programmes during the first four years of operation. It identified critical weaknesses in the implementation of a carefully planned scheme.

The primary weakness noted by Fuggles-Couchman was the inability of teachers to make the perhaps unexpectedly numerous adaptations of the practical programme to meet variations in local conditions.

Good work in one district was attributed to inter-school *shamba* (farm) competitions, and these were recommended. There was condemnation on the other hand for mission schools and others which had undertaken the cultivation of rather large areas of a cash crop to raise funds, with 'endless "shamba bashing" for small children, which could have the opposite effect to that which we wish to obtain – an interest in and keenness for farm work'.

In the middle schools, the farmwork had hardly started – Fuggles-Couchman saw only two organised farms and had heard of 'one or two' more. The standard of cultivation on demonstration plots 'left much to be desired' despite the fact that they were smaller than primary school plots – too small to occupy the generous provision for practical work in the daily timetable. There had again been a slavish adherence to the pattern of demonstration plots suggested in the syllabus: for example, one school had laid out demonstration plots on a steep hillside which should have been planted with permanent crops. Several of the demonstrations themselves also seemed inappropriate.

Following the Fuggles-Couchman report, the scheme of work in middle schools was modified to provide for more flexible adaptation to local conditions and to lessen the burden of farmwork on pupils in their examination year. Pupils in grades 6 to 8 were to share in the operation of the production farm. The new syllabus gave examples of suitable programmes for school farms of limited acreage, and insisted on advice from local Agriculture Department officials before finalising the school farm programme. These measures together with an increase in the number of agriculturally trained teachers seem to have led to some improvement in the middle school programme.

Examples of successful work were associated with the keenness of an Education Officer, Agricultural Officer, headmaster or agriculture teacher (Dodd 1969:12). They came some six years after the programme had been initiated, and at a date when the future of the programme was very much in doubt. From the beginning African spokesmen had opposed the programme, asking at a conference in England whether English educators would be prepared to introduce coalmining and textile work in their schools. The negative reaction of Tanganyikan parents to the long hours of farmwork prescribed in the syllabus was symbolised in the fate of a middle school, burned down by indignant villagers only a few months after it had been opened. This unrest was focused through the opposition expressed by the Tanganyika African National Union (TANU), which in 1954 asked the United Nations visiting missions to recommend abolition of the programme. A number of chiefs also expressed their reservations, unrest grew, and in 1957 the government agreed to comply with a visiting mission request to reduce the agricultural emphasis. After the elections of 1958 these criticisms were further voiced by TANU representatives in the Legislative Council. A new Director of Education gradually dropped the emphasis on agriculture and by 1960, when TANU members entered the Council of Ministers, gardening and farmwork had become 'merely extra-curricular activities supervised by a few enthusiastic teachers in a small number of schools' (Morrison 1976:86).

There is little information concerning the impact of the 1950s programme on individual pupils. Dodd noted that pupils continued to give preference to urban employment, however, except in the very few instances where greater earnings could be secured through cash crop agriculture (Dodd 1969:16).

Review of Strategy

The basic government strategy was to require all schools to operate the new agriculturally biased curriculum from a given date. The instructions at least were precise. All schools were to introduce the new agricultural programmes as laid down in the detailed gradewise syllabus, but making any necessary adaptations and consulting local agricultural advisers. A gradualist, normative-re-educative component was also included in the strategy, through an increase in the number of persons training as specialist teachers of agriculture for the middle schools and also through inclusion of more agricultural instruction in the preservice courses at the teacher training colleges.

The type of innovation was laid down in detail in the government syllabus. Schools where adaptation was required often ran into difficulties, however. Provision to induct practising teachers into the new programme was evidently insufficient. Human resource limitations were held responsible by Fuggles-Couchman for many of the weaknesses in the practical work undertaken by the primary schools.

A further and critical weakness was the fundamental mismatch between the objectives of the government and the objectives of pupils and their families. Since European and Asian children did not have to take time from their academic studies for agricultural work, it was difficult to persuade African parents that their children should have to do so. The labour requirements were in fact substantial. The school year was divided into two categories – 'light farmwork' and 'heavy farmwork', the latter accounting for about a third of the total.

Fuggles-Couchman considered this too long and suggested alternative arrangements by which it could be lessened and which would permit grade 8 pupils to spend more time in the classroom preparing for their school-leaving examinations. He mentioned the view that academic standards had suffered on account of restricted classroom hours. It was this that really antagonised the schools' clients. In the 1950s, African villagers were obliged to pay modest fees for their children's primary schooling (Shs. 10 per annum) and substantial fees for their attendance at middle schools (Shs. 250 per annum). In general the investment was made with the strong hope of a cash return. During the 1950s, according to Dodd (1969), it was possible for the brighter middle school pupils to earn more through working in town as a clerk, a mechanic or in small-scale industry than by working in the village, even if they had failed to gain admission to secondary schools or further education. Rural families therefore considered the time spent on the school farms as wasted, since their first concern was for pupils to do well at the school-leaving examinations to improve their chances of getting well-paid jobs in town.

As regards teacher motivation, the situation in the 1950s was such that teachers were obliged to introduce the agricultural programme. The choices before them concerned the effort that they should make to overcome problems of interpretation, and the speed with which they moved towards the more ambitious projects such as setting up a production farm. Evidence on these points suggests that motivation was not uniformly high! It would seem to have improved, however, as the more realistic proposals of Fuggles-Couchman were put into effect.

The programme might well have developed further had technical factors alone been at work. The parallel existence of three educational streams, Asian, European and African, with only the latter following the new programme, foredoomed it, however. That Nyerere proposed a not dissimilar programme before a decade had elapsed is some testimony to the relevance of the general concept to its environment. Implementation problems and client resistance persist but the research-and-development-based initiatives at Kwamsisi and elsewhere offer the possibility of a steady build-up of worthwhile 'relevance' programmes in an expanding network of innovatory schools. Progress in the agricultural education venture of the 1950s was gradual, in practice, though immediate action had been the official policy. In 1967 Nyerere called for immediate action, whilst leaving flexibility for each school to begin with self-reliance activities suited to its particular circumstances. The Tanzanian authorities since have made specific provision to reinforce the natural process of gradual improvement that may be expected where a government gives an educational programme a central place in its plans for national development.

Rural Education Centres in Upper Volta

Origin and Overt Objectives

The idea of Rural Education Centres was put forward in the late 1950s by two French administrators in the Ministry of Education of Upper Volta. In view of the difficulties of introducing universal primary education in the foreseeable future they suggested that, instead, an abbreviated low-cost course of literacy, numeracy and agricultural training should be offered to unschooled adolescents. It was calculated that if construction of primary schools was held back, some 76 per cent of boys and 24 per cent of girls could be accommodated on this course by 1970. By the 1980s, all rural youth would have the opportunity of rural education, and the course could be gradually extended to accommodate lower age groups. It was believed that adolescent pupils would be more highly motivated than primary school children and that costs could therefore be held down by condensing the rural education programme to three years. At the same time, these older pupils would be able to learn the principles and methods of modern agriculture and to offset some part of the costs of education through labour on the school farm. This alternative model was designed to provide a three-year basic education to unschooled rural teenagers combining vocational agricultural instruction with basic literacy in French and basic numeracy. It was believed that the older students would be able to address themselves to their studies more effectively than pupils of the normal primary school age, while also producing foodstuffs in the farms attached to the proposed Rural Education Centres and setting an example in modern agricultural techniques to local villagers. The very demanding objectives underlying the scheme have been summarised as follows:

> 1. to provide opportunities for *all* rural youth to receive at least a minimum of literacy and numeracy by attending a full-time school during adolescence
> 2. to inject an element of modernisation into the villages by training all young people in the basic principles and methods of modern agriculture
> 3. to lower the total cost of education for the masses by combining education with practical farm work and by shortening the total period of education during the first decades of expansion of the education system
> 4. to reduce wastage in education by concentrating the teaching on a more receptive and better-motivated age-group than that normally taken into the primary schools. (Ahmed and Coombs 1975:339.)[25]

Programme Development

The government of independent Upper Volta decided in 1961 to proceed with the idea of Rural Education Centres, but on an experimental basis. The European Economic Community provided funds for the construction of 225 centres, and over 500 centres were built using local resources (mostly by villagers using local building techniques), giving a total of 759 centres. The number of centres fell to 737 in 1972-3 but enrolments rose slightly to 24,000 – approximately one-sixth of the target figure. (Enrolments in Rural Education Centres then accounted for about one-fifth of the total school population.) The primary school building programme had not been held back – public pressure for the construction of primary schools was as irresistible in Upper Volta as elsewhere in the continent – and funds for the rural education programme were limited accordingly.

By 1973, however, the rural education programme had become so unpopular, and attracting pupils had become so difficult, that the government decided to call the experiment to a halt. The centres were transferred to the Ministry of Agriculture, for development as Young Farmers Training Centres, with a new programme of work designed to overcome the weaknesses of the earlier venture. The idea of Rural Education Centres as a substitute for primary schooling was abandoned.

A visiting mission noted some of the micro-level operational problems: e.g. that the need to introduce pupils to the language of instruction, French, consumed the bulk of the available teaching time and that the opportunity for formal instruction in, for example, agricultural methods was severely constricted. They found also that the attainments of centre pupils in respect of basic literacy and numeracy were limited. At least one half of the pupils were sufficiently weak in this respect to justify the assumption that their skills would lapse on completing the course. The same observers remarked, however, that the attitudes of Rural Education Centre pupils to rural life were more positive than those of primary school graduates, the latter being mainly interested in migration to the towns.

Review of Strategy

The government-sponsored programme was based upon a gradualist introduction of a new type of educational institution. The operational strategy and curriculum of the centres were specified by the government, but there was an element of feedback over time. The discovery that the early centres had insufficient land, for example, led to government pressure to increase the acreage provided. More importantly, the success of post-centre follow-up activities initiated by the rural education counsellor in one district led on to government recognition of this principle and the attempt to extend it more widely. Other severe problems arising from the nature of the innovation, notably the difficulties of working in French and the lack of basic agricultural equipment were not remedied in time. (The programmes initiated since 1973 offer agricultural instruction in the vernacular, operate with more adequate levels of equipment and provide for post-school co-operative farming by trainees, however.)

The Rural Education Centre innovation made heavy demands on resources and these were not always met. Land was often insufficient in quantity (1.05 hectares per centre on average in 1965-6, rising to 1.64 hectares later) and poor in quality, often the worst in the village: the impoverished villagers could hardly be expected to give up their better land. Among ten centres visited by the survey team mentioned earlier, only three had the basic implements required for the first step towards an 'intermediate' technology of farming the land of Upper

Volta and only one possessed the three 'indispensable elements' for this 'intermediate technology' – a *manga* hoe, a trained donkey and a ploughshare weeder. Practical work during the long dry sessions was limited to crafts with simple tools 'and whatever the teacher and the students can find in and around a poor village, in a country where wood is scarce' (Ahmed and Coombs 1975:345). Funds for seeds, fertilisers, repairs etc. were minimal. The farms themselves generated some funds, of course, but there was a wide spectrum of performance. In 1969-70 the 25 centres producing least output had an average income of only US $14 while the 25 most successful centres had an average income of US $340. The latter centres were presumably able to remedy any defects in their resources endowments whereas the former centres – perhaps situated in especially ill-favoured, backward areas and perhaps less competently led – could not.

The provision for teacher induction was also inadequate. Three teacher training institutes were established to prepare secondary school graduates as teachers for the Rural Education Centres. Their ten-month course included general education, agricultural theory, agricultural practice, workshop practice for boys and domestic subjects for girls, basics of pedagogy, and teaching practice – a heavy load. The teachers were expected thereafter to be able to set up a centre in a remote rural area, to establish and manage the centre's farm, maintain farm accounts, organise centre co-operatives, obtain the assistance of the villagers and act as change-agents for local development. In this they would have the support of only one rural education counsellor per district – about one counsellor per hundred or so widely dispersed centres. This proved to be excessively demanding for the inexperienced trainees.

Client Response

Villagers initially welcomed the centres as a close approximation to formal educational facilities. Later, however, as they came to realise that no certificates were awarded by the centres and that some pupils barely acquired the rudiments of literacy, they became disenchanted (Ahmed and Coombs 1975:355).

Motivation was better, however, in Yatenga district where the rural education counsellor established post-centre groups, some of which set up co-operative farms and obtained loans from banks. Continuation learning programmes were introduced, to reinforce literacy, introduce book-keeping and accounting, and add to agricultural knowledge. Some groups took correspondence courses in agricultural modernisation. Others began to diversify from agriculture towards commerce, handicraft, transportation and repairs work. The existence of these post-centre groups served further to encourage pupils and teachers within the centre themselves.

The post-centre groups in Yatenga made it possible for rural youth to put into practice some of the lessons on crop diversification and new agricultural methods learned at the centre, since funds and institutional support were forthcoming as required. Elsewhere the motivational aspect of learning new income-yielding skills was bound to be low. The rural families in Upper Volta were as poor as those anywhere, had to adhere to known subsistence crops and could not afford to purchase equipment and materials.

Teacher motivation was also poor. The difficulty of the work combined sooner or later with client apathy or resistance was a major constraint. In addition, the teacher's salary was only half that of a primary school teacher, his security of tenure limited and his housing often primitive. It was reported that teachers were often initially enthusiastic but were finally moved to despair and in some cases sought to be relieved of their posts.

A fundamental weakness was that the post-independence government remained doubtful of the merits of the French-inspired concept. The label 'experimental' was retained and the principle of low costs insisted upon, in order to minimise encroachments on the budget for the popular expansion of primary and secondary schooling. When the people voted with their feet against the programme, the experiment was finally called to a halt. The dual system of education (orthodox and ruralised) had once more proved unacceptable.

Notes

1. The most comprehensive review of the rural schools programme available in English is by Ruiz (1963); data are from this source unless otherwise stated. Brief comments on the programme are given in Myers (1965) and Tannenbaum (1966).

2. Vasconcelos had accepted the post of rector of the National University from interim-president Adolfo de la Huerta in 1920 on the understanding that he had authority to organise a system of public education. In 1921, President Obregon appointed him to head the new federal Ministry of Public Education.

3. The Regional Peasant School combined the earlier rural teacher training and agricultural training schools. Pupils were entitled to leave after the first two years to practise as agriculturalists or craftsmen. Three students out of four chose to continue their studies, however, in preparation for becoming teachers but few decided to specialise in agriculture, perhaps because of its low prestige, perhaps because they thought of moving on to employment in the cities.

4. A historical account of the development of the Village Institutes is given by Vexliard and Aytac (1964) and an account of the arguments for and against the institutes by Stone (1974). Semin (1952) also gives a concise account of the institutes' programmes. For a more general view of education in modern Turkey, with some limited material on the institutes, see Kazamias (1966). There are occasional discrepancies in dates as between different sources. Those given by Vexliard and Aytac have been cited here.

5. Nurullah and Naik (1951:558-72, 735-40). After the partition of Bengal, the government issued orders prohibiting students from participating in protest demonstrations and meetings. Some students boycotted schools and colleges while others were rusticated. A Society for the Promotion of National Education in Bengal was founded to provide for their continued education. The Calcutta Congress of 1906 further strengthened this movement by passing a resolution in favour of 'National' education.

6. Gandhi stated in his autobiography that it was reading Ruskin's *Unto This Last* which led him to the idea that 'a life of labour, i.e. the life of the tiller of the soil and the handicraftsman, is the life worth living'.

7. See M.K. Gandhi, *Educational Reconstruction: a collection of Gandhi's articles on the Wardha scheme and summary of the proceedings of the Wardha conference* (Hindustani Talimi Sangh, India, 1950), p. 28.

8. Ibid., p. 22.

9. Gandhi cited in Hingorani (1970:113).

10. The Zakir Husain Committee noted in their supplementary report of 1938 that 'this is a scheme of universal and compulsory basic education for all children, to be followed in due course by higher education for those who are qualified to receive it'. See *Basic National Education: report of the Zakir Husain Committee and the detailed syllabus* (Hindustani Talimi Sangh, India, 1938), p. 57.

11. *Post-War Educational Development in India: report by the Central Advisory Board of Education* (New Delhi, 1944). A summary of the Kher Committee's reports is given on pp. 11-13.

12. The initial report, submitted to Gandhi on 2 December 1937, incorporated outline syllabuses for the various subjects and a detailed syllabus for spinning and weaving. A supplementary report following close on the first gave detailed syllabuses for all craft and non-craft subjects.

13. Avinashilingam Chettiar, 'Birth and Growth of Basic Education (1937-61)' in *Indian Yearbook of Education 1964 (Elementary Education)* (NCERT, New Delhi, 1964), p. 64.

14. The best evaluation of the situation at school level is embodied in the report of the Assessment Committee on Basic Education, published in 1956.

15. *Education and national development: report of the Education Commission, 1964-66* (Ministry of Education, New Delhi, 1966), p. 7.

16. Ibid., p. 637.

17. Chettiar, 'Birth and Growth', p. 64.

18. *First Yearbook of Education: review of education in India (1947-61)* (NCERT, New Delhi, 1961), p. 796.

19. Chettiar, 'Birth and Growth', pp. 79-80.

20. Data for the Philippines community schools is taken mainly from Bernadino (1958). See also the profiles of representative high performance schools in *UNESCO* (1955) and Dr N.P. Pillai's comments in the Newsletter of the Asian Institute for Teacher Education, Quezon City (vol. IV, Sept. 1969, supplement pp. i-ii) on 'The Community School – Experiments in the Philippines'. See also *The Philippine Community School Training Centre at Bayambang: a joint project of UNESCO and the Philippines* by F. Fresnova, Field Director of the Centre (National Commission of the Philippines, Manila, 1954).

21. See U.H. Fleege, *The Community School: Potentialities and Needs* (Bayambang Training Centre, 1956, mimeographed).

22. *UNESCO* (1955:103-4).

23. Ibid., p. 59.

24. Principal sources for this case-study were Dodd (1969), Cameron and Dodd (1970) and Morrison (1976), together with Fuggles-Couchman's evaluation report of 1956.

25. Data from Ahmed and Coombs (1975). See also article in the *Guardian*, 25 May 1976, p. 17.

* Six programmes of relevance education have been selected for detailed study, on account of the substantial documentation available. A distinction is drawn between the power-coercive, normative-re-educative and rational-empirical approaches to planned reform representing compulsion, intensive persuasion of key personnel and general presentation of a reasoned case to all concerned, respectively. (See Chapter 3.) Some readers may prefer to proceed directly to Chapter 3 and to return to the case-studies at a later stage.

Part Two
A CRITIQUE

3 THE OBJECTIVES-CENTRED APPROACH AND ITS LIMITATIONS

This chapter comprises three main sections. First, there is a detailed presentation of the objectives cited in connection with a sample of work experience and community-related programmes. Second, there is a brief commentary on the unrealistic nature of policy-makers' statements in this respect. Finally, there is a discussion of the problems of evaluation, leading to the conclusion that it is almost impossible to discover whether, or to what extent, schools have made a durable contribution to community welfare by means of their 'relevance' programmes. The task of developing an alternative approach to the justification and evaluation of these programmes is left to Chapter 4.

Overt Objectives of Relevance Programmes

A common feature of relevance ventures is the extremely ambitious range of objectives cited in their support. The pressure of social and economic problems has led to goals such as:

1. Giving pupils knowledge and skills leading to increased productivity in manual occupations, to improvements in health, the ability to participate in village-level organisations such as co-operatives and local councils etc.
2. Conveying useful knowledge and skills to 'backward' communities.
3. Influencing pupils' attitudes, especially to create a habit of, acceptance of, or positive motivation towards, manual occupations or rural life.
4. Developing qualities of character conducive to social stability and worker productivity as well as to personal welfare, such as moral rectitude, perseverance, accuracy, creativity, self-reliance and co-operation; and where applicable, developing loyalty to socialist or other (e.g. Gandhian) ideologies.
5. Lowering the unit costs of schooling through the sale of pupils' craft products or agricultural produce.
6. Attracting pupils to school; and improving the effectiveness of the general education programme through greater local relevance, use of activities as a learning aid and as a rest from mental work.

Objectives mentioned only occasionally include the enjoyment by pupils of the intrinsic rewards of the work activities concerned and other direct benefits such as fresh air and exercise. These were seen as important by the founders of 'progressive' schooling in Europe and, in the countries of the Third World, by Gandhi among others.

Degree of Realism of these Objectives

This list could be documented ad nauseum from the six case studies and numerous other similar projects. The objectives reflect the kinds of problems confronting policy-makers in Third World countries. These problems have included low agricultural productivity, endemic disease, the absence or poor functioning of modern rural institutions, the alienation of schooled youth from the traditional styles of life and work. Is it realistic, however, to suppose that initiating in the schools a daily or thrice-weekly practice of spinning or digging or weeding or projects relating to local government or public hygiene will lead to an amelioration of these problems? Is it realistic to suppose that a well-ordered programme in the schools would produce a major transformation in the lifestyles of pupils and their families? Is it realistic to suppose that the mass of undertrained primary-school teachers are endowed with or could be supplied with the expertise in programme development, new agricultural techniques and other strategies required to meet these demanding objectives?

Cognitive Objectives

Consider first the degree of realism of the objectives relating to the transfer of relevant knowledge and skills to the pupils and through them, or directly, to the adult population. Traditional ways of life and work are bound together in a complex web of behaviour patterns not easily relinquished. These cultural patterns are derived from a world view very different from the modern one. Diet, for example, may be seen in terms of 'heating' and 'cooling' foods, or in terms of the yin-yang philosophy of the Orient. Rogers and Shoemaker (1971) illustrate this point by reference to the failure of a water-boiling campaign in a Peruvian village. In this village only the sick drank boiled water, which was perceived as retaining a 'heated' quality even when cool. If a person was not ill, he was prohibited by cultural norms from drinking boiled water. Similar cognitive structures underlying traditional agricultural practices need to be carefully researched before attempts are made to change them.

In addition, there are strong economic pressures making for conservatism in agriculture. Many farmers can ill afford the necessities for modern agricultural techniques, nor can they afford to take the risk of deviating from the tried and tested ways that provide for their subsistence.

The constraints on the possibility of school-leavers setting up as modern farmers in their own right have been illuminated by Dodd in connection with the Tanganyikan agricultural programme of the 1950s (1969:15).

School instruction in modern agricultural methods and health practices may simply lead to a dualistic system of thinking. School instruction is taken seriously as the basis for answering examination questions, traditional views are respected when in the village. Even the teachers may observe this distinction! Fuggles-Couchman (1956) noted as one weakness of the Tanganyikan programme a 'lack of conviction in teachers of what they are teaching – rarely do they apply what they teach in their own farms'. There is thus a two-stage problem in attempting to convey knowledge and skills to a traditional society by means of the schools: first, diffusing the desired new ways effectively to the mass of scattered and ill-trained primary-school teachers and second, diffusing them from the schools to the local community. Neither stage is easy. The latter, however, is susceptible to so many factors outside the control of the schools – the need for land reform, irrigation facilities, rural credit and so on, that the best efforts of the schools may bring little evident return.

Attitudinal Objectives

Consider now the objectives of developing attitudes favourable to manual work or rural life, and desirable qualities of character. It is by no means clear how the kinds of work and community-related projects that can readily be introduced into the schools would bring such developments about. Where a charismatic teacher who really believes in the value of such undertakings shares the work with his pupils, then some movement in the desired direction is a possibility. But in the more typical case, where the teacher sets the pupils to till the fields because it is government policy, does the work itself generate new attitudes?

Children from higher class families, who have perhaps had little opportunity to use their hands, might undergo some transformation of personality when they learn that their hands too could become productive and soiled. Such children though are unlikely to have to face a lifetime in the traditional rural economy. But what effect does formalised schooling in work activities have on the attitudes and aspirations of rural children, used to years of functional work? For them, school is still noteworthy mainly for the ways in which it *differs* from the life of their early years and out-of-school hours. It differs because it deals with bookwork, has a 'modern' institutional character, and leads on to national examinations. These examinations lead on in turn to modern-sector jobs, perhaps secure government jobs, several times more remunerative than rural employment, more prestigious as well, and often located in the towns. Any schoolchild can dream, while he is still on the mainstream of the educational ladder, that by hard work or good fortune he will be able to climb the ladder and obtain a well-paid job. His family can dream this too. Under these conditions it seems unrealistic to suppose that programmes of work experience and community-related studies would suffice to make him positively prefer to stay in rural employment rather than obtain a better paid job in government service or with other modern-sector employers. The possibility exists, however, that such programmes might lessen what Dore has termed the 'disappointment gap' – the extent to which life in the rural section is felt to fall short of the first preference – a government job, say (Dore 1973:5).

The arguments normally put forward in favour of work-experience programmes accomplishing at least this limited objective include the following:

- habit - the pupil maintains or develops the habit of manual work (even if he grumbles about it)
- the pupil can no longer believe that his lessons relate only to desk-work and the modern sector, as he has to engage in cultivation and craftwork also
- the involvement of the teacher in manual work may raise the status of such work in his pupils' eyes
- the demonstration that agriculture or craftwork has a scientific basis or can be studied scientifically in school may help to bring the mystique of the 'modern' world to the farm and cottage (this is related more to theory lessons and demonstrations than to regular manual work).

These are forceful arguments but are weak in the face of the ingrained attitudes, based on longstanding patterns of social incentives, that are the target of change. More pertinent is the argument that the school can demonstrate that high earnings are available from agriculture or craftwork. If, however, such earnings are available so readily that even schoolteachers usually lacking local knowledge can demonstrate the fact, while also fulfilling a heavy teaching schedule, then the local population is often likely to have learned of the situation from other sources. In any event they could soon grasp the point from the school or elsewhere, and there might be no need for a continuing school programme.

Community service projects and community studies may likewise be argued to reduce alienation through:

– reinforcement of contact between schoolchildren and the elders of the village
– introducing pupils to the challenge of social and economic development through introducing the national/international 'development' perspective
– harnessing youthful idealism through community service rather than permitting its dissipation; and so on.

Again, these are forceful arguments, but the negative consequences and unintended outcomes of 'relevance' programmes cannot be ignored. Take the case of manual work as a compulsory part of the school timetable. If the programme is seen as an imposition then peer group interaction may crystallise and reinforce incipient negative attitudes towards manual activities and occupations.

The loudest arguments against rural and manual labour have been the differentials in earnings security, styles of living and status which exist between them and non-manual employment in the modern sector. In the six countries of the case studies, evidence could be adduced in quantity to show that, whatever the moral views on dignity and nobility, agricultural and other manual work on average drew, and still draw, far lower and far more uncertain earnings than those for non-manual jobs – which are of course attained not by the 'relevant' subjects but by the academic.

Lowering Educational Costs

The objective of lowering education costs is frequently cited and presents no *a priori* difficulties. Nevertheless, given the facts that teachers are not selected as businessmen, that they are obliged to devote much of their time and energies to classroom duties, the poor resource base of many Third World schools, and the limited market openings, it would be surprising indeed if a major part of educational costs could be offset by pupil earnings.

Evaluation Studies

It has been argued in the previous section that the schools, however 'relevant' their programmes, cannot by themselves resolve the multifaceted problems of the Third World countries. Hence a statement of objectives which assumes a direct connection between adequate school programmes and the end of these problems can be a real handicap in school programme development. The teacher at the grass roots sees a condition of water shortage or landlessness as the factor holding back the welfare of the village people and is confused by the suggestion that manual work or health studies in school, or adult education programmes, could improve matters. It would be of more assistance to him if policy-makers would acknowledge the distinction between the long-term building up of a readiness for change, a process to which the schools acting on their own can contribute, and the direct confrontation of community problems, a process requiring the conjunction of several modes of social action, for example, land reform and the concerted action of a number of agencies of rural development.

One consequence of justifying programmes by referring to inflated objectives is a generalised confusion which works against effective programme development and management. A second consequence is that the evaluation of progress is exceedingly difficult. Suppose that the rural areas continue in a state of stagnation, or that educated youth continue unemployed and discontented. Does this mean that the school 'relevance' programmes should be discontinued? Have they failed? Or do they perhaps represent an improved educational experience for their youthful clients and an investment in 'human capital' that may bear its fruits ten, twenty or thirty years later? Suppose on the other hand that changes do take place – paddy is transplanted, cotton is planted with the recommended spacing, new crops are introduced, and the village co-operatives begin to function well. How is one to disentangle the contribution to this change made by school relevance programmes? Many other factors have usually been at work – radio campaigns, an enhanced agricultural extension effort, a programme of training for co-operative organisers, an improved price for farm produce, better transport facilities.

These problems may be illustrated by experience in Mexico. The early 1930s saw widespread disillusion with the results of the substantial effort to develop relevant rural schools. 'Reformers in the thirties believed that the rural school had waged a useless and uphill battle', noted Ruiz (1963:55). Too often the school had preached a message which was in advance of its time – for example, asking the people to drink water rather than *pulque* – a liquor brewed from a local plant:

> The addiction to pulque, for example, often had its roots in the waterless character of Mexico. During one of the periodic anti-alcoholic campaigns of the twenties, he (a school inspector) had

> stopped in a village noted for its pulque-drinking inhabitants. There he had called the people together and lectured them on the pitfalls involved in their use of pulque. He urged them to drink water. After he had finished, the villagers asked him to eat with them. At the table he noticed that his glass contained rancid and muddy water. Surprised and angered by this, the inspector demanded an explanation. 'Maestro', they answered, 'this is what you have asked us to drink'. For miles around, there was nothing to drink but water from stagnant pools. The people drank pulque instead. (Ruiz 1963:53-4.)

The 1930s saw an enhanced effort to provide for integrated rural development. 'Land was redistributed and then other federal departments stepped in. Communications built roads and bridges; Irrigation dammed streams and dug canals and ditches; Agriculture supplied seeds and fertiliser, technical assistance, implements and draft animals, and frequently milk cows, chickens, and pigs for breeding purposes; Education and Health provided schools and teachers, medical facilities, doctors and nurses' (Ruiz 1963:56-7). Under these circumstances, the rural school functioned in a more favourable environment but its individual contribution is hard to assess.

Evidence of a positive and enduring impact of school relevance programmes is available chiefly in connection with the work of individual, highly committed educators. The results obtained by Father Cheney in Above Rocks parish, Jamaica, is an example of a model of a school-based programme leading to self-employment in the construction trade for boys and in straw-weaving for girls. The range of programmes developed by Patrick van Rensburg at Serowe, Botswana, is another example of a successful model. In addition to training young people through cost-covering 'brigades', assistance was provided for setting up producer co-operatives, where wage employment was not available. A key characteristic of such educators is that they have *not* relied solely on the impact of in-school programmes, but have concerned themselves personally with solving initial problems and developing market outlets for ex-pupils who wished, whether as a first choice or second best, to take up self-employment, or have provided opportunities for ex-pupils to participate in community service activities. There has been no assumption that the in-school programme in itself would suffice. A further example may be cited from Upper Volta, where one particular educator – in this case a 'rural education counsellor' – developed school-leaver groups for ex-pupils of the Rural Education Centres in his district. Members of these groups, supported by him, were able to follow continuation or correspondence education, and formed co-operative units for agricultural and other activities, including commerce, handicrafts, transportation, and agricultural implement repair work. (See Ahmed and Coombs 1975: 350-1.)

These latter examples illustrate the possibilities of attaining objectives relating to socio-economic problems, through a combination of in-school and post-school programmes, but the difficulties of sustained implementation remain. Van Rensburg (1974) stresses the need for capital resources, continuing product innovation, market creation, as well as strategies to overcome problems arising from the natural and social environments. His detailed calculations show the substantial capital requirements for the 'intermediate technology' production by small numbers of people of goods which can be marketed only with difficulty.

However, because a few schools, led by totally committed educators with a high degree of managerial skill, succeed in making an impact on their immediate environment, it does not follow that such models are universally replicable. The local market soon becomes saturated with a particular skill; if schools and school-leavers are equipped with the tools to make school furniture, for which there is a large market, then adults engaged in the manufacture of school furniture and fittings would soon be out of work; if the woodworkers and their tools were, by some feat of organisation, put at the disposal of selected schools for woodwork training, then many pupils could learn woodwork but it would soon have little vocational relevance as the market for carpenters would rapidly become saturated. Problems of surplus are not always so serious in agriculture, but here land shortage, problems of transport of perishable goods to distant markets, and poor functioning of rural institutions, constitute constraints to expansion.

Conclusion

The drift of this chapter is that the objectives which have been set for relevance education and by which relevance has been justified, have been excessively ambitious. Failures to attain them spectacularly have thereby been much more discouraging than they need have been. Also, by being almost immeasurable the objectives have facilitated their own discredit. By being pursued in virtual isolation from the social, economic and political contexts of the schools, and sometimes in opposition to the objectives of the schools' clients, their feasibility has been further undermined. Finally, the frequent failure first to train the teachers adequately and then to support them fully has added to the impression that the objectives are hopelessly idealistic.

That the objectives are not intrinsically impossible, however, has been suggested by the experiences of Cheney and van Rensburg. They have simultaneously indicated that the preconditions for some success are careful articulation with the economy at large, carefully nurtured growth, superlative commitment from the educators and altered expectations on the part of the learners and their sponsors.

4 CURRICULUM BALANCE AND DESCRIPTIVE EVALUATION

A number of writers in the field of educational philosophy and curriculum studies have stressed the inadequacy of a 'means-end' or objectives-centred approach to curriculum design. Peters (1959, 1966) has suggested that education is not a 'means' to an 'end', and that attempts to specify 'ends' usually represent more or less detailed specifications of how to conduct the educational process. An 'educated' person is not some kind of pre-specified product, he suggests, but a person who has had the benefit of, or has created for himself, an appropriate series of educational experiences. The selection of a particular series of educational experiences for inclusion in the school curriculum is based on the belief that they are worthwhile activities, activities that have sufficient generality in some sense to help form the pupil's way of looking at the world, whatever it may come to be. Thus, Peters notes, 'science, mathematics, history, art, cooking and carpentry feature on the curriculum, not bingo, bridge and billiards'.

It is not necessary to share Peter's philosophy in every particular to agree with him that schooling is a process of exposing pupils to a variety of experiences which tradition and contemplation have suggested might benefit them, and that the outcome is to some extent open-ended rather than pre-specified. Pupils come from homes differing in kind and circumstances. Within each home the siblings differ one from another. Pupils enter school different and respond differently to their experiences. These experiences are moreover numerous and diverse – the formal curriculum covers a wide range of subject areas and the 'unwritten curriculum' is equally extensive: teacher-learner styles, behaviour in formal organisations, peer group interaction, and so on. It would be difficult to plot the impact of schooling on one particular student on a case-study basis, let alone *plan* in advance the outcomes for the school-going population as a whole. It may be argued that thoughtful policy-makers have long been aware of these basic facts. They have supported relevance programmes not because they saw them as a sure means to certain necessary and specific ends, but because they felt that such programmes would give *balance* to the stream of educational experiences presented to the child. This balance, they believed, would serve the child well in his personal development and leave him better prepared to face the years ahead, even to play a constructive role in the life and work of his local community, *if the opportunity presented itself*. This more modest rationale for the development of relevance programmes is logically unassailable. The only question that arises is whether schools in general are capable of developing 'relevance' work in a suitable fashion.

Stenhouse (1975) offers a summary of the debate among curriculum specialists about the place of objectives in curriculum development. He takes the view that whilst precise definitions of desired learning outcomes may be appropriate in certain contexts, they are inappropriate in fields such as the social sciences and humanities. His own experience in developing the UK Schools Council Humanities project illustrated the point. The underlying aims of this project could perhaps have been accommodated within the upper reaches of Bloom's taxonomy of educational objectives. They were of such a high degree of generality, however, that evaluation of the extent to which they had been attained by individual pupils would have been extremely difficult. It was not Stenhouse's intention to evoke a pre-specified behavioural change in each pupil. It was his intention simply to allow pupils to participate in open-ended discussion and investigation of contemporary issues, with the teacher acting as a more or less neutral chairman. The aim was in this case to support the process of value formation by each pupil in an open-ended way, without any encroachment on his autonomy in this respect. Stenhouse found that he was able to formulate a coherent set of principles regarding the selection of content and the procedures to be adopted in the classroom and that this was sufficient to guide both the work of curriculum development and curriculum evaluation. Instead of beginning with a rather arbitrarily derived set of objectives, he worked directly from an intuitively derived specification of appropriate areas of content and principles of procedure. This he termed the 'process' model (as contrasted with the objectives-centred model) of curriculum development.

Though eschewing objectives, Stenhouse worked nevertheless within a broad framework of philosophical and social values (he felt it was important to provide teenage children with the opportunity for informed and rational discussions of social issues, especially children in whose homes such opportunities were rare). It may be argued that the kinds of policy statements regarding relevance education cited in Chapter 3 likewise constitute such a framework. They provide a generalised view of the social and economic context within which relevance programmes are to be conducted, and of the kinds of problems that need to be solved. They have rarely offered a means-end view of *how* the problems are to be solved, which would require multi-agency action over a broad front, whereas relevance objectives have often been set before the schools alone. Educators have proceeded straight from their description of social ills (and their hopes that the schools may provide an avenue for tackling them) to the issue of directives regarding the introduction of new content into programmes of schooling. In practice, then, they have decided intuitively that the balance of the curriculum was not appropriate. They have decided to act unilaterally and adjust this balance, feeling that this would mean better education for students seen as individuals and some contribution to the amelioration of national problems also.

Such a policy decision is legitimate. It follows that relevance programmes should not be condemned just because some of their proponents have waxed overly eloquent about the benefits they might bring and overly optimistic about the time required for the relevance approach to yield its social dividends. The acceptance of the relevance ideal is a step towards a more appropriate curriculum content. It was noted earlier that policy-makers are likely to include both those who tend to the more optimistic view of programme outcomes and those who see the move as a step towards more effective and balanced 'general education' In Sri Lanka, for example, the pre-vocational studies programme launched in 1972 was seen by curriculum specialists as a step towards more relevant general education. At the same time, Members of the State Assembly were making public statements that this reform would solve the youth unemployment problem, or so their speeches were reported in the press. The Honourable Members were clearly unaware of the complex issues involved, for what was being established was machinery for renewing the content of junior secondary schooling. It was educational machinery, not the complex inter-departmental machinery that would have been required to solve youth unemployment. It would be wrong, therefore, to judge the pre-vocational studies programme by whether or not youth unemployment or underemployment and youth unrest persist. What is required instead is to establish whether the new programmes have reached a standard which justifies their continued inclusion as a worthwhile component of the school process.

This approach – assessment of new curricula or activities in terms of the adequacy with which schools have been able to implement them – has been developed as a complement to the 'process' model of curriculum development and has been termed 'descriptive evaluation'. It permits the immediate and continuing feedback to the policy-maker of the kind of information which will tell him directly if the programme is going badly or well (whereas evaluation of the impact of a particular school programme on village development would tax the powers of a team of highly qualified workers over a lifetime.) Most studies of relevance programmes have in fact conformed to this pattern of 'descriptive evaluation' rather than objectives-centred evaluation. They describe what is actually happening in a sample of schools, and it is left for the policy-makers concerned to use this information in deciding whether they wish to spend more time improving the quality of programmes in pilot schools, to extend the programme more or less rapidly to other schools, or to discontinue a pilot or nationwide venture.

Descriptive accounts of what has happened in a number of relevance programmes generate the following picture. *The decision to impose relevance programmes as a matter of general policy has led to a wide spectrum of performance*. At the one extreme there have been schools so innovative that their programmes have received national or international recognition as leading the way to a new interpretation of schooling. In addition, there has been a considerable body of schools where competent though often not very inspiring programmes have been developed. Then follows a long tail of schools which offer a thin and clumsy interpretation of relevance activities or neglect them altogether.

The situation in the rural schools of Mexico seems to have followed this pattern. Quite a number of these schools built up a vigorous and innovative programme of activities. These schools were able, to some extent, to fulfil the role of community uplift as well as offering an enriched programme of elementary education. Tannenbaum described the schools at this end of the spectrum as follows:

> It soon turned out that the anexos were the important part of the rural school. They included such things as a school garden, a house for the teacher, and a plot of land given to the school and worked by the adults for the purpose of providing additional income for the school or for the schoolteacher. The school also developed a kitchen where the women could learn to cook. It had a sewing machine, a barber shop where older boys cut the hair of the younger ones, and a medical kit or primitive dispensary where the teacher acted as nurse and applied iodine, bandages, and had some other simple remedies. There was no standardisation in these matters.

Each school acquired those anexos most convenient to its particular community.

The rural school came to be judged primarily not by its reading and writing but by its anexos – one school boasted of 33 separate activities in addition to teaching the three Rs. One result was that the school was always open and members of the community participated in its goings-on. Another consequence was the formation of committees of villagers to look after the various anexos: school sanitation, the school garden, the school plot, the school furniture, attendance, the night school, and so forth. The school was a busy place indeed. One teacher remarked that the school never closed. 'When I get tired I take a rest.' (Tannenbaum 1966:105-6.)

Community involvement in some locations was high and received the commendation of no less than John Dewey. At Comaltepec, the community 'built and furnished the school, planted an orchard on its ground, harvested and sold a crop of corn for the school's benefit, purchased wire for animal pens, gave chickens to the students, donated a hand loom, and provided a lamp for the adult night class' (Ruiz 1963: 38-9).

Some of the new schools thus performed well in terms of the generalised concept set before them and the limitations imposed by their environment. In many schools, on the other hand, teachers were hard-pressed to provide even the basics of primary schooling.

By the 1930s, even the founders of the rural school movement had become disillusioned by the problem of the large 'tail' of poorly performing schools. A similar spread of performance is evident from the report of the Assessment Committee on Basic Education, published in 1956. Some schools had launched substantial programmes of craftwork, with capital costs recouped from earnings in a year or so. A senior Basic school in Madras with 384 pupils had purchased equipment costing Rs.3,500 and 'in one academic year alone there was a net income of Rs.1,837'. The Basic schools of various districts of Bihar had been able to cover from 20 to 50 per cent of their recurrent costs through craftwork. But again there was a big tail.

Some evidence of a range of school performance in the Tanganyika agricultural programme of the 1950s emerges from the Fuggles-Couchman report, although this report focuses in the main on weaknesses permeating the programme as a whole.

Wide discrepancies were reported in the development of the Rural Education Centres in Upper Volta. While some centres followed the various agricultural practices recommended by the authorities, many (partly from lack of resources) failed to do so. And output varied greatly:

> The span between the low and high productivity in the centres was very wide. The 25 centres producing least had an average income of 1969/70 of only CFAF 3,529 while the 25 highest producing centres earned an average of CFAF 84,000. (Ahmed and Coombs 1975:349.)

Descriptive evaluation is never easy, and some remarks on the difficulty of such evaluation in the relevance context may be appropriate here. It is quite simple to recognise schools which have really taken the relevance idea to heart and show evidence of both quantity and quality of effort put into this work. Likewise one can recognise schools where a few seedlings have been planted and neglected, or where the pupils' alleged craftwork is scanty and evidently several years old! The problem is to generate a useful description of schools in the middle of the spectrum. For various reasons, schools are rarely doing exactly the same thing. They have different acreages of land, of different quality, different resource bases for craftwork, different relationships with the surrounding community, different proportions of younger and older pupils and so on. Are their pupils the better or the worse educated as a result of the relevance efforts? To judge this from single school visits is very difficult, yet regular visits to a sample of schools might bias their performance upwards.

There are no simple answers to these problems. The import of the chapters which follow is not to plead for massive investment in descriptive evaluation. Such evaluation, in a real life situation, tends only to quantify or substantiate one's pre-existing knowledge of seemingly insoluble programme weaknesses. The need is rather to explore new approaches to programme management, preferably approaches which have built-in elements of descriptive evaluation and improvement.

The remainder of the study represents an attempt to identify approaches of this kind. It draws upon concepts derived from the literature on the diffusion and management of educational innovation as well as on the literature of curriculum studies.

Part Three
MANAGEMENT OF THE RELEVANCE INNOVATION

5 INITIATION AND TRANSMISSION OF THE RELEVANCE IMPULSE

The main concern of this chapter is the selection of an effective general strategy for introducing relevance programmes into the school system as a whole, following a policy decision by, say, the Education Minister, in favour of this move.

A number of authors, writing in the 1960s, described three main approaches to planned organisational change. The best-known formulation is that of Chin, who distinguished power-coercive, normative-re-educative and rational-empirical strategies.[1] These categories are almost self-explanatory. A *power-coercive* strategy for change relies for its effectiveness primarily on the authority of a government or other body to enforce its own policy decisions. The *normative-re-educative* strategy is interpreted mainly in terms of the various forms of 'sensitivity training', designed to render persons or groups holding key organisational positions more sensitive to the need for ongoing organisational change. The *rational-empirical* approach is characterised by the assumption that demonstration of the intrinsic merits of an innovation will lead to its adoption where appropriate. Dalin (1973), in his review of a range of innovation programmes in OECD countries, noted that government policies in education are often implemented by drawing upon more than one of these approaches. He substituted the term 'political-administrative' for 'power-coercive' as being more appropriate to educational policy-making. This term is used here also. He further used the term 'normative-re-educative' in a slightly broader sense than might be used by a group dynamics specialist and in the chapters which follow it is used more broadly still.[2]

The categorisation provides a useful framework for analysis of the broad strategies adopted in different countries and at different points in time for the relevance innovation, for the introduction of work-and-community-related programmes in the schools. It is true that elements of more than one approach were present in the majority of programmes. Nevertheless, for the purposes of exposition, strategies may be classified as leaning more heavily on one such approach than another. The remainder of this chapter is devoted to a consideration of the circumstances leading to the adoption of a particular strategy for programmes falling within the three broad categories – and to a consideration of the advantages and disadvantages ensuing from the choice of strategy in each case.

The Power-coercive or Political-administrative Approach

The power-coercive or political-administrative approach has been dominant in the programmes reviewed for this study. It has taken different forms depnding upon national circumstances. Three important subcategories in this respect are (i) the mandatory adoption of relevant education by a set of new educational institutions from the time they are established (e.g. by rural schools being established in a country where rural schools were previously lacking); (ii) the mandatory adoptionof relevant education programmes by all or most members of a school system that is already well established, within a special short period of time; and (iii) government-sponsored programmes designed to bring about gradual or stepwise or partial introduction of relevance programmes in a school system that is already well established.

Mandatory Adoption of Relevant Education by a New Set of Educational Institutions

The most clear-cut examples in this category are the rural schools programmes of Mexico and Turkey. In both instances, the rural areas lacked facilities for rural schooling and were considered backward in respect of agricultural practices, health practices, social organisation etc. In both cases, a revolutionary or reformist government decided upon a programme of rural schooling designed to transmit knowledge and skills relevant to community uplift (to boht pupils and their elders) as well as literacy, numeracy and the orthodox school subjects.

The particular strategies adopted in Mexico and Turkey were somewhat different, however, reflecting different social conditions. In Mexico, the rural schools movement was initiated by recruiting a group of 'missionaries' – young urban-educated supported of the revolution – who visited the rural areas, recruiting teachers locally from among the small number of literate rural people. These teachers were informed of the multiple roles expected of the new rural schools, and in-service training sessions were arranged for them. Substantial problems were encountered, however. The in-service training sessions fell short of what was needed both quantitatively and qualitatively. Many teachers were obliged by government policy to offer relevant education to children and adults, but had to undertake this challenging task without external support. (Pre-service training programmes were also initiated but many of those trained as rural teachers preferred on graduation to take up employment in the cities.)

Popular pressures in post-revolution Mexico necessitated the speedy *ad hoc* provision of rural schooling. In Turkey, on the other hand, there were less of these pressures. Indeed the rural population was to some extent antipathetic to the concept of modern schooling, its spokesmen referring to the lack of practical utility of what was taught in schools. There was also a loyalty to the concept of education as the study of Koran and of the Islamic traditions. In these circumstances it was possible for Atatürk's government to draw up careful plans to establish practically oriented rural schools around trained personnel. An abbreviated agriculture-centred course of training was initiated first, in 1935 (with rural primary graduates studying for six or seven months on government 'model farms', where some general education courses were also provided for them). A five-year course of secondary education combined with teacher training, again for the graduates of the existing rural primary schools (it was believed that urban youth would not adjust to rural life), was introduced two years later, with the founding of two 'normal schools' for villages, known after 1940 as Village Institutes. The number of institutes was increased to 14 in 1940 and rose to 21 in 1948. Students spend half their time on academic studies and half on the study of agriculture and rural crafts. On graduation they were legally obliged to remain as village teachers for 20 years (or repay the cost of their training). And they were legally obliged to undertake the education of the community as a whole in modern agriculture, crafts, home management, co-operative organisation etc. The government was, however, legally obliged in its turn to supply the teacher with the materials he might need – agricultural and craft equipment, livestock, seed, young trees etc.

The Turkish programme combined the coercive power of the law with the normative-re-educative concept of a five-year preparation for the role the Village Institute graduate was to play. Data on the actual operation of the rural schools are limited, but it seems likely that this combination of approaches was fairly potent. Certainly the Village Institutes came to be seen as all too effective in exerting a radicalising effect on the younger generation, and with the advent of a conservative government in 1950 they were closed.

A further example is the establishment of the Rural Education Centres by the Upper Volta government which accepted on an experimental basis the plan for condensed courses of relevant basic education – to be offered to unschooled rural teenagers. Teacher training centres were established, albeit offering only a brief (ten-month) course of study in general subjects, pedagogy, agricultural science, agricultural fieldwork and workshop techniques. RECs were founded as trained teachers became available and reached a peak total of 759 in 1971. However, despite having sole responsibility for a complex educational institution, these teachers were paid less than teachers in the country's primary schools.

The experience of Upper Volta, even more than that of Mexico, points to a recurring weakness of government policy in the field of relevant education. This is the tendency to use the authority of the government to launch a programme for which the necessary resources, knowhow, organisation and public support cannot be sustained. In Upper Volta, unlike Mexico, it was possible to hold back the pace of expansion to the rate of production of modestly prepared teachers. The REC concept, also ensured that some agricultural work was done whereas in Mexico many rural schools fell short of the community development concept altogether. Lack of resources and lack of public support undermined the REC programme completely, however, and the concept had to be abandoned.

These examples show already that although a government may appear to be free to initiate a relevance revolution on the basis of its own authority, it is unlikely to succeed in its objectives unless it is prepared to tailor its edicts to the prevailing circumstances; and that haste, as in Mexico and Upper Volta, may not result in speed. These lessons emerge with even greater clarity from the history of attempts to achieve immediate universal implementation of relevance programmes throughout an existing school system, as delineated in the next section.

Mandatory Adoption of Relevant Education by All or Most Members of a Well-established School System Within a Specified Short Period of Time

A number of important programmes have been launched on the basis of immediate universal adoption by the schools. This policy has reflected in part the urgency of political pressures. Contributing also to the adoption of this policy has been an insufficient awareness of the constraints on what even a government can demand – a lack of understanding of the complexities of the process of educational innovation. The balance between these two factors cannot be established unless one has an 'inside' account of the decision-making process.

The agricultural programme for African schools in the Tanganyika of the 1950s may be cited first, as a well-documented account of a policy of immediate universal adoption. Here the political pressures in favour of immediatism were not acute, although the apparent alienation of primary-school leavers from the land was causing anxiety. A rather different factor contributed to the choice of policy, however. The structure of rural schooling was to be changed from a six-year course of primary schooling to a four-year course at primary school followed by a four-year course at middle school. It was decided that the transition to the new school structure should coincide with the introduction of the practical bias into the school curriculum. Hence the syllabuses issued for the new four-year primary and middle schools included specifications for classroom studies and practical work in agriculture to be undertaken by pupils in each grade. The schedules for practical work leaned heavily on the experience of one particular agricultural research station but schools were instructed to adapt these proposals to local circumstances, drawing upon the advice of agricultural extension officers where necessary.

Under these circumstances, each rural school in effect took on the status of a 'pilot' school, experimenting with curriculum materials as yet not fully tested. Yet the teachers lacked entirely the feeling of service as pioneers and the sense of collegiality with professional curriculum development workers that have sustained pilot-school teachers in more recent times. Isolated, and sometimes without adequate reference materials, they encountered real difficulties in coping with the obligations that had been imposed upon them. Some teachers failed to understand the concept of experimental plots, which was fundamental to the primary school fieldwork. Teachers, and likewise supervisors, were unable to adapt the lessons and crops to the region (Fuggles-Couchman 1956:3,8).

The logic of Fuggles-Couchman's arguments is that agricultural programmes would be best worked out jointly by consortia of neighbouring schools, since they could more effectively obtain the advice of an overworked agricultural extension officer, could pool books and agricultural knowhow, and through discussion might figure out how to adapt the local guidelines to the particular plots of land available at their own schools.

Returning to the question of national strategy, it is clear from Fuggles-Chouchman's report, that schools often instituted ineffectual agricultural programmes, being obliged to act on the basis of specifications that had not been adequately tested out on a pilot basis and without an adequate basis of agricultural knowledge. Improvement *was* possible – as Dodd (1969) has reported. One may observe that here, as in other programmes, the government's determination to institute agriculture as the *key feature* in the school curriculum, for *all schools at once* had proved impracticable. The number of schools offering adequate programmes could only rise gradually, as feedback was obtained, local adaptations were evolved, the stock of teachers with agricultural training was increased (pre-service training of primary-school teachers was also given an agricultural bias in the 1950s), and good ideas or correct practice were diffused through formal or informal channels from one school to its neighbours. Government *fiat* could not override the time-consuming process of bringing together the various elements – resources and skills, knowhow based on experience, and communications (structured or otherwise), needed for programme installation.

The evidence of this case-study already indicates the fundamental weakness of the policy of 'immediate universal adoption'. Yet it must be realised that the establishment of a set of pilot schools which offered an agriculture-centred curriculum while other schools offered an academic curriculum would have been unacceptable to the rural folk concerned (see Chapter 8 below). Alternatives *are* available – pilot ventures superimposed upon an orthodox curriculum, for instance, but these alternatives lack appeal to the policy-makers unless they have become fully sensitised to the constraints imposed by the problems of educational management on their freedom to initiate system-wide educational change.

Tanzania provides a more recent example of the policy of immediate universal adoption. Nyerere's call in 1967 for the introduction of production programmes in all educational institutions, as part of the new approach to national education is set out in *Education for Self-reliance*. The lessons of the 1950s were well taken. *All* pupils were to participate in self-reliance activities. Also, schools were to enjoy *total flexibility* in the design of their production programmes – thus avoiding the problems associated with the 1950s pre-specified schedules for demonstration plots and for the middle-school production farm. A further asset was the fact that some staff had experience, either as teachers or pupils, of the earlier agricultural programme. Nevertheless, the basic problems posed by a strategy of immediate universal adoption could not be avoided. While all schools had by 1968 introduced production programmes of some kind, the quality of these programmes ranged from excellent through to disappointing. As regards the ideas, or principles of procedure, set out by President Nyerere – such as training in democratic procedures, community orientation and reliance on hard work and local resources – many teachers were unable to translate these ideas into concrete operations:

> Many teachers responded to the call by urgent staff meetings at which *they* decided what the school effort should be and proceeded to organise the pupils accordingly. Some, in true capitalist fashion, drew up grandiose plans for carpentry workshops, irrigation schemes, chicken batteries, or tractors, and sought financial support that they should have known would not be available. Only a minority of teachers involved the local elders and officials in discussion . . . and integrated the effort of the school with that of the community . . . One immediate problem is to persuade the experienced teacher of the new political and sociological significance of what he does and says in school.[3]

In-service training programmes were instituted with the objective of accomplishing this transformation. Nevertheless, the magnitude of the innovations proposed by Nyerere in *Education for Self-reliance* became steadily more evident, as feedback data illustrated implementation problems, and the 1970s saw the introduction of a supplementary gradualist strategy for curriculum and teacher development. (New curricula, evolved at pilot schools associated with the College of National Education, are to be introduced on a stepwise basis throughout the country.)

Documentation is available to show that Tanzanian educators were well aware of the management problems of the self-reliance innovation. The political pressures arising from a sudden expansion in the number of dissatisfied primary-school leavers in 1965-6 had led the Education Minister to acknowledge the case for agriculturally-oriented schooling and 'a bandwagon effect was soon apparent among middle level politicians who expected immediate and extensive implementation of curriculum changes, particularly those involving practical farming'. Despite these pressures, a gradualist strategy had at first been decided upon:

> Educational administrators kept emphasising to the Minister and his Cabinet colleagues that it was more important politically to do the job well: a large-scale programme with untrained teachers and inadequate materials and implements would merely regenerate the hostility of the 1950s and produce demoralising confusion among teachers. Despite some reluctance among political leaders, it was agreed to introduce an experimental programme by slow stages, beginning in 1967 with a Standard V course in agricultural theory and only fifteen full-scale pilot school farms. (Morrison 1976: 208-9.)

The worsening of the primary-school leavers crisis in 1966, the National Service dispute in October 1966, and the economic crisis leading to the *Arusha Declaration on Socialism and Self-reliance* in February 1967 and accompanying nationalisation programmes, created a situation in which the Education Ministry's strategy was no longer tenable. Rather, the President seized the opportunity presented by Arusha and the consequent measures to work towards a change of focus throughout the education system as a whole, through publication in March 1967 of *Education for Self-reliance*.

The Ceylon of 1965 and the Sri Lanka of 1972 also provide examples of mandatory or near-universal adoption. The Senanayake government elected in 1965 immediately embarked upon a work-experience programme in which schoolchildren were required to participate in the paddy cultivation campaign. Almost a million pupils each year worked in the paddy fields at weeding and transplanting, out of a school population (composed mainly of the younger age groups) of just over two million. In a way the concept was simple and the problems were organisational. Some aspects of the programme were unpopular – pupils getting their uniforms (sometimes their only ones) dirty, missing their lessons, and having to face the scorching sun and the chill monsoon rain both in the paddy fields and at rallies held to celebrate work-experience achievements. Nevertheless, the programme continued undiminished for the life of the Senanayake government. Due to its straightforward nature it *was* to some extent susceptible to government *fiat* – though whether it had any beneficial effect on pupil attitudes is a very different question.

The political associations of this work-experience programme led to its discontinuance by the Bandaranaike government, which came to power in 1970 pledged to develop its own concept of basic education. Following the youth insurrection of April 1971, public opinion moved against the 'colonial' heritage in schooling (the orthodox school subjects were assumed to have alienated young people from rural occupations). Senior Education Ministry personnel felt that proposals for the gradual or voluntary introduction of a more relevant curriculum, though offering many advantages, would miss the flood-tide of opinion favourable to change. They felt also that the gradualist approach would generate criticism – some children being required to follow new relevant curricula while others were permitted to follow established and recognised courses of study leading to the General Certificate of Education examinations. The public was expected to be more tolerant of the wide variation in school performance which would inevitably accompany the early years of a policy of immediate mandatory adoption. The policy-makers were right, in that the anxieties of 1971 permitted the introduction of 'pre-vocational studies' as the dominant subject in the curriculum for junior secondary pupils without much public protest. They were right too in anticipating a wide range of performance in the early years (although all schools presumably made some effort to generate adequate programmes by 1975, when the first cohort of pupils had to sit a paper in prevocational studies as part of the new grade 9 junior secondary-school leaving examination). The policy-makers had to face a less satisfied public from the end of 1975, however, when parents felt that their children had failed the pre-vocational studies examination as a result of variations in programme quality and assessment of classwork between one school and another. This unease, coupled with a change of government, brought pre-vocational studies to a virtual end in 1977.

Government-sponsored Programmes Designed to Bring About Gradual or Stepwise or Partial Introduction of Relevance Programmes in a School System that is Already Well Established

The cases cited in this section refer to government-sponsored programmes designed with a longer time-horizon or with no definite commitment to system-wide reform. There have been and are no doubt many programmes of this kind which go unheralded, e.g. the introduction of workshop studies or home economics classes into a certain number of schools each year as funds are allocated for construction of specialist rooms and as specialist staff become available. This is a case of gradualism with respect to practically oriented resource-intensive courses which are already well established.

Gradualism in respect of innovative relevance programmes has sometimes reflected the desire to conduct pilot studies and proceed on the basis of experience, has sometimes reflected the desire to achieve high standards, and has sometimes reflected the reluctance of administrators to go ahead with the relevance programme. In the case of Gandhian Basic Education, all three factors made their mark. The Zakir Husain Committee of 1937 proposed a gradualist strategy with an emphasis on the need for both experimentation and the urgent introduction of teacher training programmes. They did not specify any time-horizon for complete conversion of schooling to the Basic pattern but indications of their thinking were the suggestion that states should provide for all teachers to attend orientation courses in Basic Education within five years, for selected rural areas to be given a full complement of schools, all on the Basic pattern, within five years, and for teacher training schools to be converted immediately to the Basic pattern and their graduates assigned to new Basic schools or to existing schools being converted to the Basic model. There was to be gradual conversion of 'compact areas' to Basic Education.

It was suggested that with a determined school-building programme and the Gandhian principle of cost-covering, craft-centred education, free and compulsory seven-year Basic Education could be introduced in the course of twenty to twenty-five years – by about 1960. Unfortunately, due to the war, the independence struggle and partition, the first decade was almost lost. Pilot institutions had indeed proved themselves but against this, Basic Education's foremost advocate had been assassinated. Senior educational administrators began to evince a lukewarm attitude to Basic schooling but often justified their position by reference to the costly equipment required for craftwork. The Assessment Committee of 1956 attributed the slow progress to administrators' stalling, and noted that the policy of compact areas had become an instrument of retardation rather than progress.

The slow grinding of the wheels of policy did have some impact. New Basic schools and Basic teacher training schools were established over the years, and by 1963-4, just before the policy of Basic Education was discontinued, there were some 7 million pupils enrolled in Basic schools outside Uttar Pradesh. This figure constituted only some 15 per cent of the 46 million pupils enrolled in primary and middle school classes outside Uttar Pradesh, however.[4] In effect, while unwilling to speak out against Gandhi's educational legacy, senior educators withdrew from the concept of mandatory extension of Basic Education. Gradualism thus came in the end to reflect a power struggle between advocates and opponents of Basic Education rather than a strategy for reform.

Gradualist programmes centred around particular institutions of teacher education might also be cited here. They merge, however, into the next category of implementation strategy, the normative-re-educative approach, and are left for discussion under this heading.

The Normative Re-educative Approach

Thus far we have considered implementation strategies in which the motive force was primarily the government's authority to order change and the obligation of principals and teachers to obey the orders they received. This approach has serious weaknesses. Not least is the fact that in a widely dispersed education system, with infrequent visits of supervisors to the schools, principals who are antagonistic to reform can circumvent the government's instructions, pleading lack of resources, delays, or lack of suitable staff. Another weakness is that the reforms may be implemented in a superficial way and without understanding or conviction on the part of the teachers – which transmits itself to the pupils.

Awareness of these problems has led in some instances to the adoption of a strategy designed to generate commitment to the relevance philosophy as well as the technical competence to implement it. Mere addition of courses in agriculture and health to the curriculum of existing training colleges is unlikely to generate the necessary commitment. The same may be said of attendance at brief courses of in-service training. Two approaches which may, however, generate this commitment are (i) the development of an innovative pre-service teaching training programme, and (ii) the involvement of serving teachers in the process of course development.

The Village Institute programme in Turkey is an example of strategy (i). The concept of a 50 per cent allocation of the prospective teachers' time to practical studies and of their helping to erect new institute buildings may be presumed to have generated a special kind of orientation on the part of the trainees, as would their courses in rural economics and co-operative organisation etc. More importantly, it may be presumed that some of the personnel appointed to these institutes were convinced advocates of Ataturk's philosophy, even though many staff were transferred from the earlier 'normal' schools which were run down at this time. At any rate, enough Village Institute graduates became 'radicalised' to threaten the sense of security of the elite.

An early example of this teacher-centred approach from the British experience, documented by Griffiths (1976), was the teacher training and materials development centre at Bakht er Ruda in the Sudan. The college offered a course of secondary education initially two years in duration, later increasing to five years. The founder-principal, V.L. Griffiths, brought with him the ideas of child-centred, activity-based progressive schooling as well as the concept of curriculum 'ruralisation'. He took pains, however, to adjust his plans to the requirements of an Islamic culture and to the values of his fellow staff. He saw the limited appeal of farmwork to both staff and students and contented himself with requiring students to undertake some agricultural work organised by themselves as members of a student-producer co-operative. Relevance he sought mainly through the generation of a complete new range of school readers, teachers' handbooks etc. All Bakht er Ruda staff were constantly engaged on this course development work, trying out new approaches in the classroom etc., and the aims they were seeking to achieve seem likely to have been transmitted to the trainee teachers. Novel features of their course of study, such as the project approach to environmental studies, and the near absence of examinations would have also given the sense of participating in something new. The experience of studying at the college, supplemented by teachers' handbooks for use once working in the schools, support by Bakht er Ruda staff during their annual school visits and in-service training at the college on a continuing basis enabled them to make their contribution to the introduction of more relevant education in the course of a decade. Regular in-service training of school principals and teachers, to introduce the new teachers' handbooks, created a receptive climate for the new graduates, as did the fact that the institution which had trained them was responsible for setting the primary-school leaving examination.

More recent ventures in which pre-service teacher training has been linked with course development work include the IPAR (*Institut de Pédagogie Appliquée à Vocation Rurale*) in Cameroon, the Namutamba project in Uganda, the Kwamsisi project in Tanzania and the Bunumbu project in Sierra Leone. In such instances, it seems likely that college graduates will see the relevance aspect of their training as important because it has been associated in their minds with high-level curriculum development experts (rather than low-status agricultural and craft instructors, as at the ordinary training colleges). Unfortunately the task of preparing the schools to receive the new graduates graciously is much harder than in the Sudan of the 1930s. Dispersed throughout the vast primary school systems of today, the trainees will encounter pressures to conform to the conservative educational philosophy of the existing teaching force. (Bakht er Ruda trainees of the 1930s entered a school system of only a hundred or so institutions, each in direct contact with Bakht er Ruda.) The problem is similar to that of the business executive who returns from his 'sensitivity training' as a new man with new ideas but who finds his fellow executives unreceptive and loses heart.

This problem has led in the world of business to the practice of providing sensitivity training for groups of executives from one particular organisation rather than for groups comprised of individuals from a number of different firms. The corresponding strategy in the world of curriculum development would be to concentrate training on teams of teachers working together, in pilot schools for instance. Here the curriculum development worker in his visits to the schools not only conveys useful technical advice to the teachers concerned and inspires them with the spirit of innovation but does the same for the school principal and, where applicable, community members. The members of this team tend to develop a sense of identification with the spirit of the innovation.[5] There is no formal documentation of this phenomenon for relevance innovations.

It is suggested here that the normative-re-educative strategy may usefully be interpreted in the context of the relevance innovation as requiring intensive and prolonged contact between teacher or teacher trainee and some committed relevance workers: either in a college committed to innovating work in this field or in the pilot school type of venture. It is suggested further that the effectiveness of this strategy would be much enhanced if the random dispersal of would-be innovators could be avoided. Some ways of doing this are discussed in later chapters.

The Rational-Empirical Approach

Governments have rarely relied on the rational-empirical approach alone – the putting of a reasoned case – as the basis for introducing relevance programmes into the schools. In some instances, however, they have supplemented a reasoned case with incentives – such as the offer of grants – rather than compulsion. The introduction of 'earn-and-learn' programmes in Rajasthan (India) was on this basis, for example. In other cases they have used the rational-empirical approach as a supplement to compulsion – in almost every relevance programme some attempt has been made to explain the rationale underlying the programme as persuasively as possible, though governments have often neglected the equally important task of showing, through concrete examples, that their proposals are workable and what they mean.

The rational-empirical approach taken alone has been more typical of initiatives 'from below'. The Philippines community school and barrio high school movements began with the espousal of relevance concepts by educators in the provinces. The efforts of Patrick van Rensburg in Botswana provide a further example. His concept of 'brigades' for the education and training of primary-school leavers was taken up on a wider basis through his advocacy of the merits of the system.

The rational-empirical approach is an apparently weak tool. To introduce work experience and similar programmes, new resources have to be acquired and teachers and principals have to acquire new skills. Community members have likewise to be convinced that the programme does not threaten the *private* interests of their children. Many school principals would hesitate to introduce a work-experience programme, for example, if the government merely publicised the merits of the programme without making it compulsory. Even though the school principal might see the merits of the programme also, without compulsion he might be unable to gain the co-operation of teachers and parents. This is the reason why governments have so often had recourse to the use of compulsion. The rational-empirical alternative – building up a climate of public and teacher opinion in favour of more relevant programmes – is laborious and success cannot be assured. This alternative, combined with the normative-re-educative approach to generate a nucleus of committed teachers, should nevertheless be considered.

This brief review emphasises the role which compulsion has played in the introduction of relevance programmes and some of the limitations of this approach. Normative-re-educative and rational-empirical approaches taken on their own have their limitations also. The upshot of the present discussion is thus not so much the definition of one 'best' approach but the need for the educational planner or administrator to make a conscious decision regarding how these approaches might best be combined. One view is that the core of the strategy must be the progressive build-up of committed personnel through the normative-re-educative strategy. Where possible, the government might use its administrative powers to shelter the work of these innovators and permit diffusion of their work based on 'contagion' of the re-educative spirit and rational-empirical appreciation of their work. Governments are not always in a strong enough position to follow this gradualist policy, however. Where a policy of immediate universal adoption is unavoidable, then normative-re-educative strategies for building up committed workers and rational-empirical strategies for gaining the support of educators and the community at large are needed also.

Notes

1. See Chin and Benne (1967). Chin (1967), summarised in Hoyle (1970), showed the parallelism between the various typologies.

Chin	Jones (from Etzioni)	Miles	Walton
Power-coercive	Coercive	Power-solution	Power
Normative-re-Educative	Normative	Relationship-attitude	Love-trust
Rational-empirical	Utilitarian	Problem-process	Problem-solving

2. For present purposes 'normative-re-educative' is taken to mean a substantial personal involvement likely to create a sense of identification with a new approach.

3. From the report prepared by a senior administrator in 1968, cited in Morrison (1976:280).

4. These figures apply to pupils enrolled in grades 1 to 8. Basic schooling after independence was divided into Junior (grades 1 to 5) and Senior (grades 6 to 8)

stages. ('Post-Basic' schooling was also proposed but only a few such institutions were established.)

5. See the observation that schools which participated in the experimental phase of the Nuffield science projects subsequently served as nuclei for the diffusion of these projects (Rudd 1973:39).

6 THE KEY INNOVATION: THE CLIENTS' EXPERIENCE

Thus far we have considered the policy decision regarding the basic posture of the change agents in a relevance programme – whether they are to stand as spokesmen for something compulsory, as agents of conversion through close personal contact, as exponents of a rational programme for action, or as more than one of these. We come now to the more detailed planning of a programme for action – to the delineation of the change-agents' strategies. It is not possible in a comparative study and with limited data, to delineate each innovation system in detail. The characteristics of the chain of communications in the government-sponsored programme typical of the relevance area will have, instead, to be sketched out in a more general fashion. More needs to be said, however, about the nature of the relevance programme in the schools – for two reasons. The first is the obvious one – that these activities are the kernel of the present study and need to be described. The second is that this very question is often passed over with the assumption that it is a mere technicality. The severe constraints on the range of activities that a given school can initiate – and the importance of the way in which these activites are approached – are often ignored.

A problem of sequencing arises at this point. It might seem logical to consider first the communications systems among educators, for example, the chain of transmission from Education Minister to the teacher in the schools. On the other hand, the actual sequence of policy-making is rather different. The questions are, what is required of the pupils (or adult clients) and, second, how can the education system be activated to bring this about? This latter sequence is adopted here. Accordingly, we proceeed now to consider the type of innovation introduced in the schools. The characteristics of innovation systems designed to bring about this process are discussed subsequently in Chapter 7.

The characteristics of the relevance programmes introduced into schools may be discussed under two headings: (a) the content area and (b) principles of procedure.

Content Area

We begin with the selection of activities relating to the world of work, followed by activities relating to health and other areas of community life. The important point to emphasise here is the magnitude of the task set before the schools. The *problems of organising productive activities for each child in a school or grade with tens, hundreds or thousands of pupils are immense*. This point is commonly overlooked by policy-makers and accounts for many past failures and present weaknesses in this sphere.

Agricultural Activities

The difficulty of providing regular experience of productive manual work for large numbers of pupils may be illustrated first by reference to agriculture. The situation of Cuba illustrates, through contrast, the problems faced elsewhere. The scheme of 'schools to the countryside', initiated in 1966, provided for older pupils to spend about seven weeks in the countryside in school camps, undertaking such work as harvesting coffee, weeding etc. Here the structure of the economy generated seasonal peaks in labour demand which could be turned, with big inputs in terms of organisation, to the cause of work-oriented education. And again, the new 'basic secondary schools in the countryside' provide for an enrolment of 500 pupils and for an acreage of farmland of no less than 500 hectares. The land is cultivated by pupils and teachers (for three hours a day) with a few full-time workers to assist and supervise the pupils' work. A hectare of productive land per pupil! The schools are residential and during the vacation pupils' relatives visit the schools and spend two hours a day tending the farm, so that continuity of labour supply is maintained. The initial investment for these schools is high but, as noted earlier, the value of agricultural output is expected to cover recurrent costs, and should pay off capital costs in a decade or so.

Contrast the situation elsewhere. Frequently, schools have been expected to achieve educational miracles with a few acres, or a fraction of an acre of land, sometimes land so unpromising that even hard-pressed villagers had been unable to obtain a worthwhile return. Note, for example, the problems of the Rural Education Centres in Upper Volta: 'counsellors of rural education are unanimous in their comments on the quality of soil: too many villages have given the worst possible fields to the rural education centres . . . The hectarage allocated to each centre is generally too small . . . The centres are for the most part inadequately equipped' (Ahmed and Coombs 1975: 335-64).

The average land allocation per centre was 1.6 hectares (estimate for 1969/70), to be cultivated jointly by 45 adolescent trainees. Lack of suitable land was a major constraint on the development of agriculturally biased school curricula in Tanganyika during the 1950s. A number of middle schools were unable to build up a production farm of the kind prescribed in the syllabus (4 acres under cultivation, 4 acres fallow and 12 acres of grazing) (Fuggles-Couchman 1956:6).

Fuggles-Couchman stressed the need for a flexible programme which could be adapted to the conditions prevailing in different parts of the country and to the resource endowment of the school. Nyerere adopted the same policy in *Education for Self-reliance*, suggesting that teachers, pupils and the community should consult together to design appropriate ventures. Though consultation was sometimes neglected, this general flexibility did permit schools to design programmes appropriate to their own situations and resources. The size of the garden or *shamba* was limited by the amount of empty land near the school, falling between the one-acre *shamba* at a school in Dar es Salaam and a twenty-acre farm at a school near Iringa. Achievements depended not only on the acreage of land but on qualitative factors also.

Two successful Gandhian 'post-Basic' schools in Gujarat, shared the characteristic that their founders had been able to obtain tubewells from the government. In this way they were able to establish flourishing farms on land (about 50-100 acres per school) which had previously constituted only poor-class grazing land. *Schools in those areas which lacked a tubewell could have undertaken only very limited agricultural programmes*. The Gandhian workers were also dedicated and well connected enough to obtain any supplies and equipment they required, through government grants or private donations.

It would seem then that agriculture may be a viable activity for pupils in certain geographic locations, where some or all schools have access to good and well-watered land and where arrangements can be made to cover weekends and holiday periods. Equally it would seem that in many Third World schools agriculture can never be a major production activity for the pupils, because the acreage of good or passable land is insufficient. And in most schools there will be seasons when no agricultural work whatever is in progress. *This suggests that a scheme for pupil activities based on agriculture may often leave many pupils seated at their desks for most or all of the year*.

These problems undermine both the idea of giving the pupil a significant experience of productive work under school auspices, and the idea of using the school as a means of introducing modernised agricultural techniques to rural communities. The latter objective requires, *inter alia*, sufficient land and a budget such that relatively expensive inputs can be purchased in sufficient quantity and in good time. Such conditions have rarely prevailed in Third World school systems, though they have sometimes prevailed in individual schools.

Higher and Lower Technology Craft Activities

Gandhi perceived solutions to those very problems. He wanted village pupils to do agriculture as part of their school work. But he also identified spinning as a handcraft that could be undertaken daily by every pupil in every school, when there was no work in the fields. One of his first concerns on returning to India in 1915 had been to find a spinning wheel and a spinner. After some time neglected spinning wheels were discovered by a woman colleague in the attics of some peasants in Baroda state. Gandhi likewise sought out the experience for hand-carding of cotton and for hand-loom weaving. This research proceeded well enough for Congress to pass a resolution in 1920 in favour of hand-spinning and hand-loom weaving and in the years that followed Gandhi gave much personal attention to building up the Khadi movement. In consequence, by 1937, when the idea of Basic Education was launched, India had a reservoir of skills and expertise in this sphere, and Gandhi could assert with confidence that primary school pupils could pay for their tuition by spinning if the state would guarantee to purchase their products.

India now has a complete spectrum of technology in this sphere. Pupils in the Gandhian schools of today use the small spinning wheels in the lower grades and take their turn at the more complex *ambar charkas* in the higher grades. The younger pupils likewise use simple manual devices for ginning and carding the cotton, while the older pupils use the pre-processed material needed for the *ambar charka*.

Attempts to introduce Basic Education on a large scale faltered nevertheless, not least due to difficulties in implementing the craft-work programme. Though Gandhi had mentioned education centred around the hand spindle, the Zakir Husain Committee's syllabuses required very heavy outlay on a wide range of spinning, weaving and ancillary equipment. Perhaps partly from lack of equipment, they failed to produce yarn, cloth or other craft products, in quantity or quality sufficient to cover any substantial part of their operating costs. Gandhi's spinning programme does, however, illustrate certain pre-requisites of a production-oriented craft venture, viz. a *local resource base* (cotton), an *appropriate (low-cost) technology*, and, in principle, *market potential*. These three factors are vital to the success of school production programmes, and that was what Gandhi sought, both from the viewpoint of meeting the costs of schooling and training young people to earn a subsistence.

Health

Health was an important feature in many of the early campaigns to raise the level of living in isolated rural communities. Following the Hampton-Tuskegee tradition, health and hygiene were stressed in the Phelps-Stokes reports and the British policy of 'adapted' education that followed them. As noted in Chapter 3, the good intentions of reformers often met with a limited response, since rural folk often saw their health and dietary traditions as adequate to their needs and since these traditions were often an integral part of the local world view. (See for example, Wilson 1963:41-4).

One of Wilson's observations was that villagers accepted the community service rendered by the students – cleaning, tree-planting etc. – with a good grace but without any sense of the need to undertake similar activities themselves. Such experiences make one question the durability of the impact that the Philippines community schools had on the community health practices. Health was a principal feature of the schools' campaigns, and achievements at the time were considerable, as indicated by the following statistics for the early 1950s (even if some degree of over-reporting is allowed for):

	No. of health-related projects	
	1950-1	1953-4
Garbage collection	4,499	20,053
Toilet construction	9,800	25,486
Model house construction	2,913	7,915
Establishing health centres		2,828
Drainage improvement		13,510
Child and maternity care		2,218
Food demonstrations		3,098
Other	3,683	6,394

Health education was a principal focus of the general science and civic training syllabuses laid down in the Zakir Husain Committee's scheme for Gandhian education and pupils in grades 6 and 7 were expected to 'undertake an active health campaign in the village'. Health projects featured also in the Mexican rural schools programme, and in nuclear schools set up elsewhere in Latin America.

In recent times health education for school pupils has tended to be integrated with the general science curriculum, and the health education of adults entrusted to other agencies. The theme of a direct role for the school in community health does recur, however, as in the specification that the 'ruralised' school of Cameroon should present a model (with latrines, a clean water source etc.) for emulation by the adult population.

Past experience suggests that schools have only limited potential for community leadership in this sphere. The teacher has neither the expertise in health matters or in community development techniques to fulfil this role, and the community resists the involvement of children in cleaning work etc. as well as the idea of changing community habits.

Other Community-oriented Activities

The community schools of Mexico and the Philippines paralleled the American concept, which embraced many fields of human endeavour. Activities in the Philippines included building schools or classrooms, reading centres, bandstands, playing fields, community centres, libraries, museums, bridges and roads; beautification of the locality by planting tress and shrubs; initiation of boy and girl scout groups and 4-H clubs. In many instances the schools attempted work with adults, introducing the idea of neighbourhood groups with elected committees, as well as adult literacy classes.

Batten (1959) gave some idea of the range of activities undertaken under British auspices. Under community service he cited 'Kashmir Labour week' and the annual work camps held in the then Northern Rhodesia. In his comments he pointed out that such community service projects typically required little skill and at best served to assist in the character development of the pupils concerned (and to assist in that only if pupils, teachers and community members found the idea well conceived and the projects well organised). Regarding work with adults he commented that the community may tire of a series of 'projects' suggested to them by the teacher, just as the teacher may run out of ideas. He stressed too the overload on the teacher imposed by adult education and community development work and commended the alternative concept of getting parents to take an interest in the work of the school. In principle, he noted, the school could provide a continuing focus of interest for the community, though in practice many teachers are unwilling to involve community members in this way.

Community involvement was very much a part of the Gandhian concept and pupils were expected to assist at village festivals and so on. The Zakir Husain Committee laid much stress also on the national and local relevance of the social studies programme, much of which focused upon 'civic training' and study of local community institutions. Committee members were familiar with the activity methods and project-based study favoured by modern educators and saw the relevant social studies curriculum as providing a vehicle for such approaches. (The village teachers were unfortunately some way behind them and remained uncertain of what the committee had in mind.)

Taking an Integrated and Flexible View

So far, has been noted the range of relevance activities attempted by the schools and some of the problems associated with each. The separation of these activities for purposes of exposition should not, however, be taken as an indication that schools ought to choose between them. Rather, it would seem desirable for schools to have the maximum of flexibility in arranging a sequence and mix of relevance activities to match the seasons, the occurrence of festivals, the initiation of campaigns by government, the changing needs of the community and the changing composition of the school staff. These activities may further be assimilated, to a greater or lesser degree, to the more orthodox programme of studies – thereby enhancing the value of such studies as well as placing the practical activities in a meaningful perspective.

These suggestions may seem obvious but their implementation is fraught with difficulties. Experience indicates that a circular instructing schools to follow such an approach forthwith would lead to widespread confusion and neglect. Such recommendations in fact imply something of a gradualist strategy, with those to whom they are meaningful pioneering a path which others may later follow. Furthermore, they imply governmental support for such innovation, which can otherwise fall foul of red tape and direct opposition. (See Chapter 8.)

The organisational burden imposed by activities of this kind has frequently been underestimated. There is a strong case for the appointment of a teacher with a much reduced teaching load responsible for the external relations of the programme. In some instances the school principal has taken this role and made arrangements for the purchase of materials, sale of produce, and participation in community life. Where the principal's load is too heavy or where principals in general are not very forward-looking, this role might best be shared between the principal and a specially designated teacher. The latter would play a key role in supporting the constructive activities of ex-pupils, if an attempt were made to build upon the relevance programme by the creation of post-school groups.

Principles of Procedure

The principles of procedure specified for relevance programmes derive in part from the values of the authorities, as implicit in their statement of programme aims, and in part from their assumptions regarding clients' behaviour and attitudes. They may derive also from the experience of educators who have been asked to give substance to the outlines of policy laid down by the authorities.

Too often it has been assumed by the authorities (political or educational) that simply getting children to work with their hands, tilling the fields or cleaning up the village would accomplish a transformation of attitudes in favour of manual work and rural life. As pointed out earlier, the psychology underlying this assumption is naive. Rural children are mostly *used* to working with their hands. Moreover they and their parents may believe it is *wrong* to waste precious study time on such work. The results are then hardly likely to be those intended. There is ample evidence, from the 1920s to the 1970s, that under such circumstances the principal outcome is that the philosophy advanced by the authorities falls into disrepute.

What principles of procedure can be identified then, to ensure that relevance programmes are experienced more positively and provide a beneficial learning experience for their clients? Some basic principles derived from the literature are cited below. The list is by no means comprehensive and represents merely a first attempt to identify prerequisites for the development of meaningful programmes or alternatives that may be considered in the process of programme development.

Principle 1. Explaining the Rationale of the Programme to the Schools' Clients, and Enlisting Their Sense of Idealism, Where Appropriate

This principle does not perhaps apply to the youngest pupils but is very important for older ones. It may present real difficulties where the relevance programme has been planned from a central office. The administrator who insists the restlessness among school-leavers can be avoided if pupils are 'made to work with their hands' presents a problem here for the teacher whose pupils regularly absent themselves at peak agricultural seasons to help their families with the harvest or clearing the land for planting. 'Acquisition of useful knowledge and skills' is a rationale which can present the teacher with problems also. There are a few instances where the teacher has new practical skills at his disposal which rural families are in a position to take up and which are not available from other sources, such as agricultural extension officers. (In many instances school gardens have been 'objects of ridicule' (Wilson 1963:43) for their poor siting and mismanagement!)

Where a national philosophy has been developed which incorporates the idea of rural uplift, the task of explaining the rationale of a relevance programme may be easier. Basic Education, for example, was conceived as one component of a multi-faceted programme for rural reconstruction and the Gandhian philosophy continues to provide support for it where it survives. Likewise in Tanzania, *Education for Self-Reliance* provides a text from which an understanding of the philosophy underlying the self-reliance production programmes can be derived.

Learning to do something well, learning about different aspects of community life and work, learning to work carefully, learning to co-operate with others, participation in the development effort, and community service, are among the possible reasons that might be advanced in justification of relevance programmes of various kinds. In principle, pupils ought to be encouraged to talk things over and clarify for themselves the ways in which they might expect to learn from and ought to co-operate with a relevance programme. The teacher is not advised to do this, however, if there is a danger of mass dissent! Patrick van Rensburg, a fairly charismatic personality, came to be so much at odds with his secondary-school pupils over the question of voluntary manual work on Saturday mornings that he finally resigned from his post as school principal over the students 'elitist' attitudes.

Failure to discuss the rationale of the relevance programme at all can lead to disastrous misconceptions. An elementary pre-vocational programme may be construed as having the objective of conveying marketable vocational skills. Alternatively, the pupils may work out the rationale for themselves on the basis of day-to-day observation. Interviews with pupils have elicited the responses that relevance activities are undertaken to impress important visitors or to make money for the school. They may also be seen, correctly or incorrectly, as a device for making money for the teachers!

Principle 2. Involving Pupils in Planning and Administering the Activities

The same activity may be seen by pupils as an imposition, if they are simply told to do it by a teacher or as a privilege, if they are allowed to undertake it in school-time, as members of a producer co-operative who can look forward to sharing in the proceeds. Participation in the planning and administration of a work-experience or community service activity can give it a meaning – through identification and improved comprehension – which renders it interesting and significant rather than merely dusty and sweaty. One benefit is thus a more positive attitude to the activity itself. Another is the experience gained in planning, co-operation, administrative procedures, book-keeping, taking minutes etc. which could have a useful carryover into adult life. If pupils can participate in the selection of relevance activities as well as their planning and execution, these benefits are likely to be enhanced.

Principle 3. The Teacher to Share the Work

Experience suggests that where a teacher is prepared to share in pupils' efforts, then pupils are better able to appreciate the benefit of what they are doing. Where teachers relax in the shade while pupils labour in the sun, or where the teacher leaves pupils to look after themselves during a craft period, not caring whether they achieve anything or not, then the activity is downgraded in the pupils' eyes.

Principle 4. Interest and Reward of the Activities

A weakness of some programmes is that they are highly repetitive. The broad field of textile crafts – seen by Gandhi as a possible foundation for a Basic school programme – was transformed in many schools into daily or occasional spinning on a *takli* (hand spindle). Agricultural education has likewise often deteriorated into manual labour without motivation or understanding. Cameron and Dodd (1970:69) noted of the adapted education policy in Tanganyika, for example, that 'agricultural education of some kind was imparted in all schools at all levels, although as often as not it degenerated into mere manual labour on large non-typical holdings to supplement fee revenue'.

One way of stimulating pupil interest in work-experience programmes is to ensure that they receive some or all of the fruit of their labours, in cash or in kind. Teaching new income-yielding skills, and the provision of follow-up support for school-leavers, may also be mentioned here, though they present major problems of implementation. These approaches are discussed at greater length in Chapter 8 which deals with client motivation.

Principle 5. Small Group and Individual Projects

Not much has been written about the use of the project approach in relevance activities. Clearly some individual or class activities, such as each pupil making a doormat or the class constructing a health centre, could be defined as projects. The implication behind the phrase 'use of the project approach' is somewhat more specific, however. It is that pupil interest and attention should be engaged in a rather personal way by encouraging one or several pupils to develop a plan of investigation or action that is their own in some sense, and that differs from what other pupils are doing. There is an element of self-direction and open-endedness that adds to the range of learning experiences and permits the exercise of creativity or divergent thinking.

No doubt the best teachers everywhere have been able to work on these lines. Of systematic attempts to implement this approach, one may cite the home projects undertaken by pupils in the Philippines community schools and barrio high schools, and at Comilla in East Pakistan, now Bangladesh. Dr Pedro Orata has given examples of substantial projects undertaken in the Philippines and his writings provide a source of inspiration in this respect. Where voluntary participation in the relevance programme is acceptable, then this approach is a good one. Compulsory home-based projects are rarely successful, however, because the teacher is unable to ensure that all pupils are conducting these projects as required. (See Batten 1959.)

The project approach is in fact difficult to operate in respect of compulsory, system-wide programmes. The work-experience programmes so carefully developed in Maharashtra, India, for example, were specifically presented in the context of the project approach. Evidence from pilot schools indicated, however, that teachers often proceeded in more orthodox fashion, giving theory lessons, followed by instructions for class exercises. It has been argued that teachers tend to adhere to traditional classroom styles in this way because of an unwillingness to change their habits. Such unwillingness may well be present. But a sufficient explanation of slow progress towards the project approach is often the low level of capitalisation. In the case of a work-experience programme in electrical crafts, for example, schools which are able to purchase only a few sets of components for the simplest electrical circuit would be unable to support a project approach. It might be argued further that some relevance activities do not lend themselves well to the project approach. Maintenance and repair of equipment scarcely does so. Where an aesthetic or investigative element is involved, however, creative initiatives by individuals and small groups may be possible. The use of local materials as the basis for work-experience activities in the artcrafts represents a case where the project approach might be possible at low levels of capitalisation.

Principle 6. The Maximisation of Pupil Choice

A closely related matter is the place accorded to individual pupil choice. It is surely a feature of human nature that one comes to identify more with activities which one has selected for oneself. Choice may in some instances be exercised in respect of participation in a relevance programme (as at Comilla or the earn-learn centres in Rajasthan) or in respect of undertaking activities additional to the collective school programme (as with home projects in some schools in the Philippines).

Voluntarism is not appropriate or politically feasible in many relevance contexts. Even the provision of the most modest choice between activities often seems difficult. It may be, however, that teachers are unaware of the desirability of allowing pupils some freedom to select relevance activities related to their interests and needs. One pupil, for example, might be interested only in making brushes that he could sell, while another pupil might see fibrework as providing the opportunity for self-expression through the creation of free tapestry designs.

Principle 7. Guiding Pupils Towards Self-direction and Co-operation (Rather than Competition in the Context of Formal Assessment)

Worthwhile relevance programmes should be sufficiently viable that pupils' attention should not have to be elicited through examination requirements. The argument is based on the belief that examinations in relevance subjects will tend to distort and ossify the presentation of those subjects, working against the benefit that they are supposed to bring. Where relevance activities are to feature in a national examination, then note-taking and stereotyped practical exercises will be given pride of place, and open-ended exploration of a range of activities ruled out. Examinations also stress the relative performance of the individual, pitted against his peers (or sometimes, bizarrely, the contribution of an individual to the very artificial co-operative effort of a group). Practice in genuine co-operation towards practical ends (co-operation arising from within rather than the knowledge that marks are being given for it) would, however, be more relevant to the rural development process, which is often as severely retarded by mutual distrust and unwillingness to co-operate as by anything else.

Principle 8. Use of Local Resources

The use of local resources was a suggested theme for the Sri Lanka pre-vocational studies programme, along with the study of local occupations. The suggestion proved a productive one and many schools were able to develop interesting courses based on the development of new uses, or a wide range of uses, for local fibres, woods, clays, bamboo etc. The policy decision to include pre-vocational studies in the junior secondary-school leaving examinations led to a decision to treat the use of different resources as different course options. Where relevance courses are not examined, a wider mix of local resources can be used.

The Maharashtra work-experience programme, in contrast, being derived from a different philosophy, did not follow this principle. The philosophy in respect of technical subjects was to introduce pupils to small-scale service activities that represented a growth sector in the economy. Hence topics such as electrical repairs, stove repairs, radio repairs etc., were to the fore. It was hoped that some pupils might later develop businesses in this sector, while other pupils would derive specific benefit from an awareness of how to maintain their own stoves, electrical equipment etc., as well as the generalised benefits of a work-experience programme.

Principle 9. Teaching Theory as Well as Practical Work

There has been a wide divergence of policy in this matter. Obviously pupils should be given an adequate explanation of what they have been asked to do. There are reports of pupils conducting agricultural operations without understanding, however, and this is taking the manual work element too far. The real question is whether teachers should be required to give formal instruction in the theory underlying agricultural, craft, health-related and other activities. Some educators have argued that teaching theory should tend to generate respect for the activity concerned, by putting it on a par with orthodox school subjects. They have suggested further that theory teaching should facilitate the transfer of learning to a wider context. As against this a requirement for formal theory instruction may militate against the development of a flexible and vigorous programme. In some cases, schools have had to discontinue the secondment of boys to wayside garages for practical work experience because neither the garage staff nor the schoolteachers were able to conduct parallel theory lessons on motor mechanics. Likewise a teacher may be disinclined to explore an unfamiliar field if obliged to give theory notes on it. The school principal may also discourage the choice of a topic on which only one particular teacher can give notes, since there is always the substantial risk of the teacher being transferred to another school mid-course.

Principle 10. Correlation of Relevance Activities With Orthodox School Subjects

This principle has attracted many supporters. Gandhi's original conception of Basic Education was that all studies should be 'correlated' with pupils' craftwork. The Zakir Husain Committee developed an example of a primary school curriculum correlated to textile crafts. It suggested that the natural and social environments should also be used as centres of correlation. Many teachers had difficulty in devising convincing modes of correlation between the lessons they wanted to give and the proposed centres of correlation and examples of meaningless 'forced correlation' have been cited in the literature. Correlation of this kind has been advocated repeatedly – for example, by Orata in the Philippines, for the Tanganyika 1950s agricultural programme, for the 'education for self-reliance' programme and the Sri Lanka pre-vocational studies programme.

In recent years it has been realised that such correlation presents too great a challenge for many Third World teachers, given their limited formal education and especially their lack of on-the-spot reference facilities. It is realised that correlated teaching requires back-up in terms of teachers' handbooks and teaching materials, prepared by educators with access to reference books and subject-matter experts as well as experience in curriculum development. The Kwamsisi project in Tanzania is an example of teachers and curriculum development workers having co-operated in developing a model integrated curriculum correlated with village activities and self-reliance production programmes.

The span of relevance activities likely to be undertaken by most schools in a particular country is relatively finite. It would be of value therefore if booklets, or entries for a loose-leaf folder, could be made available in the local languages for different relevance topics, to introduce the basic theory and correlation with other subjects (as well as practical techniques) to village teachers with no other source of reference. In this way, teachers could more effectively undertake such theory teaching or correlation as might be required of them or which they might deem appropriate.

Principle 11. Involving Pupils With Local People and Outside Experts

One problem that arises when children receive much more formal education than did their elders is that the natural social links between the generations become more difficult to sustain. One principle of procedure which has frequently been advocated is designed to reinforce these links. It is for the school and its pupils to interact more closely with the adult members of the community. Such interaction has been difficult to achieve in practice, however. Teachers have with some effort been persuaded to lead their pupils forth into the villages to undertake community service projects, but these have not necessarily involved adult community members except as spectators. Teachers have been willing to allow adult education classes to be held in the schools and have been willing to teach them (especially if paid accordingly); but these have often been completely divorced from the classes for children. Teachers have accepted parent-teacher associations, where these have concerned themselves mainly with raising funds, but here again the children may have been little involved. What teachers have not been very good at is stimulating direct interaction between children and adults. Some attempts have been made – for example, children teaching adults to read, and holding certain of the children's relevance classes in the village so that interested adults can attend (as at some community schools in the Philippines).

Often, however, the exhortation to entice local farmers, fishermen and craftsmen to help with work-experience programmes has been unproductive. Some observers have argued that teachers are not yet sufficiently confident to see themselves as managers of an educational process but prefer their earlier role as the fount of all school knowledge. Often, their argument runs, the teacher may be unwilling to acknowledge that the illiterate farmer or craftsman has expertise which he, the teacher, lacks. The teacher's problems are considerable, however, and it may be that such problems, as much as status considerations, have been a hindrance. In the first place it may be difficult to select particular members of a farming community to offer comments on farming methods – since other members of the community might well object to the teacher's choice. Then again the teacher may suspect that the explanations given by a traditional farmer will be based on a world view that conflicts with the modern science in the school syllabus. Such a contradiction might seem fascinating and stimulating – a starting point for discussion – to the educator with a PhD in soil chemistry, but would be distinctly unwelcome to the teacher with a middle-school leaving certificate or an 'O' Level qualification in general science. Another problem is that an outside aide may require payment for his services. Another is that conventional timetabling may result in relevance periods being scattered throughout the week, rather than concentrated in a way convenient to an outside resource person.

Experience in Sri Lanka suggested that these considerations were indeed important. While schools made only modest headway in utilising the human resources of the local community to enrich the pre-vocational studies programmes, they were quite willing to recruit outside personnel for school-based ex-pupils' training courses. Significant factors here were the fact that a salary was payable for teaching these courses, that time-tabling problems were negligible as they were held after school hours, and that the courses were specifically oriented to practical skills and were unexamined. Hence the problem of non-teachers having to provide 'notes' was avoided.

Kale[1] has emphasised the importance of 'field orientation' and contact with technical experts in connection with her review of the pilot stage of the Maharashtra work-experience programme. While acknowledging the practical and financial difficulties faced by teachers in organising class visits to factories, farms etc. and in contacting outside experts, she suggested that such activities were a necessary complement to in-school exercises, especially where school facilities were limited. She noted the greater pupil involvement in schools where an ex-pupil, a pupil's father or others had given technical help that brought the level of competence in the work-experience programme to within sight of professional craftsmanship.

The case cited by Kale of an ex-pupil engaged in stove repair work who assisted with work-experience classes in stove repairs suggests a possible area of middle ground between requiring teachers to work with adults and no involvement of skilled outsiders. This is to draw upon the services of young people, perhaps ex-pupils, for assistance with practical work. The in-service training and course development centre operating at Kandy, Sri Lanka, over the years 1973 to 1974 made use of this principle (though here the 'students' were practising teachers). Young people who had acquired traditional craft skills in ceramics or wood-turning, for example, came to the centre as demonstrators in return for training in design from the centre's director and their travelling expenses. School-leavers also served as aides in return for multi-craft training. The possibility that teachers might find it easier to work with young 'experts' recently out of school rather than members of the adult community would thus seem to merit consideration. While providing a link between community skills and the school programme it would not, however, provide a link across the generations. It may be that other subject areas, such as social studies (oral history and village surveys), would provide a more easily manageable basis for building such links.

Note

1. Dr (Mrs) Kale, private communication, and Kale (1973).

7 INNOVATION SYSTEMS AT OTHER LEVELS

What innovation systems should be established in order to ensure that an adequate concept of the relevance programme is developed and is transmitted throughout a school system? A chain of communications, human and printed, must link the policy-maker with the school principals and teachers whose task it will be to implement the policy (and if possible these communications must flow in two directions, not merely from centre to field).

Often the chain has been too frail. Written exhortations or the issue of detailed syllabuses suffer from the drawback that many principals and teachers cannot digest an abstract or complex document and translate it into action. Nor, for many, does it supply the necessary motivation. Face-to-face contact is needed, though alone this too has its limitations. Personal interaction, supplemented by reference materials and guidelines, is required in appropriate form for each link of the chain, supplemented, where possible, by access to examples of successful relevance programmes already functioning. If the programme is to be mandatory for all schools, then this multi-stage, multi-media change system must reach all schools, with provision for feedback data regarding its impact. If the programme is being conducted on a stepwise voluntarist basis, then suitable 'messages' would again need to be sent to the schools in general but full support would only be required for participating schools.

Few relevance programmes have achieved this degree of planning. Hence the poor standards of performance in many schools need cause little suprise. One venture which did, for a limited period, enjoy relative success was Bakht er Ruda, and the factors underlying this success were significant. Key factors were the institution's considerable autonomy, and the small number of government schools in the Sudan at the time – only a hundred or so in the 1930s. Griffiths, the founder-principal focused equally upon printed and human resources in the task of converting primary schooling from narrow rote learning to relevant, pupil-centred schooling based on understanding. Noting that there were no materials to support the teaching of anything but rudimentary literacy, he began by developing textbooks, readers and teachers' guides. In the attempt to make these relevant to the country, acceptable to national sentiment and religious belief, and workable in the classroom, he fell well behind schedule. The net result, however, was the creation of a bulky series of publications designed to provide complete support for the teacher working in an isolated village with no other reference facilities or teaching aids. A parallel programme of in-service and pre-service training was instituted, and the new materials were issued only to teachers who attended these courses. The small number of schools made it possible for the entire cadre of teachers to become acquainted in person with Bakht er Ruda and its approach, and for college staff to visit each school during the period set aside each year for this purpose. Under these conditions the college was able in the course of a decade to introduce an environmentally oriented curriculum incorporating some practical work in handicrafts, and to make a beginning in the introduction of project work. When conditions changed, however, it was difficult to maintain this level of performance. Rapid expansion of school provision in the later 1940s and thereafter caused the rapid promotion of experienced teachers and the recruitment of untrained staff in large numbers. Much of the ground that had been gained was lost, as Bakht er Ruda was unable to maintain its network of direct communications with the vastly increased number of schools. Some benefits of the 1930s programme remained, however. Griffiths concluded, after a brief visit in 1970, that the development work incorporated in the printed word – the handbooks etc. – was still bearing fruit decades later.

Introducing the Relevance Innovation

We turn now to the situation where the central authorities face the task of introducing a relevance innovation into a large population of schools. The following aspects or elements of the innovation systems devised for this purpose may be considered: (a) reliance on central or decentralised initiatives: central system for devising programme content *versus* decentralised systems for programme generation *versus* a combination of these; and (b) communications chain: systems for

- research and development work at the centre and in the field
- induction of supervisory and advisory staff
- induction of pre-service teacher trainers
- induction of in-service teacher trainers
- pre-service teacher induction
- induction of principals
- induction of serving teachers.

These systems are considered briefly in turn.

Responsibility for Programme Structure and Content: Reliance on Central or Decentralised Initiatives

One approach to the innovation process has been to set up a temporary innovation system at the centre to generate specifications for the programme and then attempt to transmit the fully specified programme through one or more channels of communication to the schools. The programme may be drawn up on the basis of 'received knowledge' by one or more experts or may be evolved through an initial period of experimentation. The original specifications for Gandhian Basic Education were drawn up by the Zakir Husain Committee and its consultants in a matter of months (though the various Indian states prepared their own schemes at a later date). Some observers have commented on the tendency to adhere closely to this specification even where it was not entirely appropriate e.g. the emphasis on cotton-spinning even in areas where cotton was difficult to obtain.

In the agricultural programmes introduced in the African schools of Tanganyika in 1951-2 a centralised procedure for programme formulation was adopted. The syllabuses were adapted from 'the syllabuses drawn up by J. Heberton for the training of teachers' (Fuggles-Couchman 1956:1). They drew extensively upon the experience of one particular agricultural station (at Ukiriguru) which was of limited applicability in other parts of the country.

In some instances, institutions engaged in curriculum development have provided the authorities with syllabus specifications, teaching materials and teachers handbooks for system-wide implementation. The development of an environmentally oriented curriculum at the IPAR in Cameroon followed this pattern. The four sections of the institute provided an integrated system by means of which the bare policy decisions of 1967-8 were translated into many tons of materials for issue to the schools (teacher training being provided at the same time) (Lallez 1974). The experimentally evolved syllabus for community-oriented schooling developed at Korogwe College of National Education and Kwamsisi village school in Tanzania may serve the same function as the community school approach is extended.

An intermediate strategy, combining centralised and decentralised development was followed in Sri Lanka over the period 1972 to 1975. This experiment began with a phase of central specification regarding programme structure and with decentralised programme development. In the initial phase of the pre-vocational studies programme schools were informed of the broad philosophy underlying the programme, of the curriculum time allocation, and of the manner in which this time allocation was to be subdivided. Schools were strongly encouraged to develop their own locally relevant programmes though they were permitted, if they had the necessary resources, to offer instead the well-established pre-vocational topics which had previously been available (in some schools) on an optional basis – agriculture, home science, woodwork, metalwork, weaving, ceramics and commerce. Teachers developing new programmes were required to submit their course outlines to the Curriculum Development Centre in Colombo for comment and advice.

In many relevance programmes there has been no centralised direction regarding the details of structure or content and schools have had flexibility in respect of programme development. The Mexican rural schools programme followed this pattern, and flexibility was a characteristic also of the 'nuclear school' approach adopted elsewhere in Latin America. Among more recent ventures, the self-reliance programme in Tanzania initially followed this model, and the 'continuation' programme in selected middle schools in Ghana is likewise based on the circumstances of each school. The 'production' orientation of Zambian schools is again locally adapted.

A further approach to innovation may be mentioned finally as combining centralised initiative and flexibility. This is for the government to designate one or more institutions to have responsibility for open-ended exploration of the relevance approach. The Jeanes School in Kenya for training itinerant teacher-educators in community-oriented schooling is an example. Its first task was to develop a locally adapted 'message' and its second, to devise appropriate ways of disseminating it. UNESCO-backed experimental programmes at Namutamba Teacher Training College in Uganda and Bunumbu Community Teachers College in Sierra Leone typify the open-ended approach where exploration is the brief and where the mode of dissemination of the results is left for consideration when the time is ripe. The second IPAR centre in Cameroon, at Buea in the anglophone region, has likewise followed an open-ended approach, again with UNESCO backing.

The view taken here is that whether or not a central specification of programme content is used in the interests of speed and convenience, there is a continuing need for programme upgrading based on the creative powers of the teacher force as a whole. Even for a modest relevance programme, it is a long haul to the target of good or satisfactory programmes in all schools. Moreover, the concept of relevance implies continuing innovation. The environment changes (modes of production, health facilities and problems, employment opportunities) and so do the schools' clients – in the knowledge they gain by informal means, in their world view, their family situations and their aspirations. Such changes are best registered at the grass roots. There would seem to be a strong case for research and development work here and also at central institutions specifically designated for the task. These two types of research and development therefore feature in the message chain discussed in the rest of this chapter.

The Communication Chain: Generation and Transmission of the Relevance Impulse

We now consider the innovation systems at various stages in the generation and transmission of innovation systems. These systems vary according to the general strategy adopted and the provision for centralised or decentralised programme development. We begin by examining the resources and priority accorded to research and development work in support of the programme.

Research and Development. This function has typically received little attention. Reasons for neglect have included the effort to launch a new system, the relevance innovation, with minimal resources, or an emphasis on speedy nationwide reform. A further contributory factor has been the lack of recognition that launching a relevance programme in schools is a complex and demanding operation. It has been too easily assumed that agriculture and craft activities, for example, being the province of illiterate peasants, can easily be taken up by teachers from a very different social background, adapted for use with the hundreds of pupils in a school, and correlated with ordinary subject teaching.

However, launching a programme of research and development in this sphere, without much previous experience of comparable work, is not easy. In India, for example, it was recognised from the start that the concept of Basic Education would need to be elaborated on the basis of experiment and developmental work. Specific provision was subsequently made in the first Five Year Plan for the development in each state of a model institution in which Basic principles would be worked out through action research from kindergarten to college. The authors of the Five Year Plan progress report for 1953-4 noted, however, that there had been 'much delay' in starting these projects and that none 'can as yet be said to be fully functioning'. The problem of an inadequate elaboration of the Basic concept generally and inadequate development of guidelines for Basic schoolteachers in the interpretation of key terms such as the activity approach to teaching, the correlation of orthodox subject matter with craftwork and the natural and social environments remained to the end.

Research and development work is facilitated where time pressures are not too severe. (This alone is no guarantee of progress, as evidenced by the Gandhian experience.) Thus at Bakht er Ruda, research and development work included the collection of teaching materials from all parts of the Sudan, the production of visual aids and illustrations by college illustrators, the preparation of trial lessons and their evaluation in the college practice school. All these activities preceded the printing of the finalised teaching materials. This development work took many years longer than expected but since the programme was conceived on an ongoing basis, the delay could be accommodated. In contrast, development work has sometimes been programmed to precede the launching of a new curriculum in the schools – to be completed within a predetermined period or on a fixed date, and its effectuality has been impaired. In the recent Cameroon reform, for example, staff responsible for research and course development were constrained by the tight schedules for the mass printing of schoolteaching materials (Lallez 1964:65). Something of the same structure obtained in Maharashtra, India, where the research and development effort was strong during the pilot phase of the 1970s work-experience programme. Plans were laid for an ongoing programme of research and development work thereafter but resources were not available to sustain this. In contrast the research and development effort linked to the 'education for self-reliance' programme in Tanzania followed after the launching of the programme – a situation which has permitted an open-ended approach without undue constraints of time.

The Sri Lanka pre-vocational studies programme has been mentioned as providing an important example of development work taking place at both centre and periphery. At the centre – the Curriculum Development Centre in fact – a small pre-vocational studies group attempted to develop guidelines for the schools, publishing booklets regarding programme construction in general and course outlines for prototype topics such as the coir industry and coir work. This group proved too small for its work, however, for in addition to consultancy work in person with selected schools, its members had to work through the course outlines sent to them by several thousand schools, service the teachers' panels which prepared course outlines for the eight topics finally decided upon, and prepare for a national examination to cover the pre-vocational studies area.

In this instance, innovative schools experimented with new uses for local materials and developed courses on this theme. Regional directors of education and their staff also in some cases undertook development work, as did inter-school committees of teachers in certain districts. The pre-vocational studies centre set up by the Director of Education for Kandy district was especially noteworthy. Much more could have been achieved, however, had more resources been made available for development work – in particular, if there had been a larger team at the Curriculum Development Centre and/or systematic provision for developmental work at the regional level. A conflict does, of course, arise between the deployment of innovative young staff in the schools and in full-time support work. And school posts are already budgeted for, while ancillary posts are not.

Viewing the relevance literature as a whole it seems that the need for research and development work has been consistently underestimated. This is true even of work at the centre. It is even more true in the field. Even where the relevance programme is relatively narrow in scope, teachers working in isolation may find difficulty in interpreting it creatively. Thus the Maharashtra work experience programme required teachers to offer a course lasting only one semester, at no more than three periods a week – a course for which they had had two weeks of full-time preparation and for which they had been issued with teachers' handbooks. Many teachers nevertheless felt a lack of confidence in teaching work-experience courses which were new to them, or found it difficult to interpret the programmes in the circumstances of their own schools. This is the same kind of problem that beset the 1960s generation of curriculum development programmes in the West. The case for inter-school co-operation in programme development and application on the lines suggested by Rudd (1973) should accordingly be considered in respect of Third World relevance programmes also. This would enable teachers to pool their ideas regarding particular problems, to adapt programme proposals in the light of their common experience and to generate new ideas more practicable or rewarding than those with which they started. Support by a district or regional development officer would help here, as would provision to cover such items as travelling expenses. Morale and effectiveness would be further improved by extensive reportage of such local development work in some form of journal or newsletter. The concept – a rather broader one – of the teacher as researcher (Stenhouse 1975) might also be explored wherever teachers with an appropriate background or researchers willing to involve themselves can be found. The idea here would be to study more deeply the processes that actually take place during work experience or community-oriented activities, and on this basis to develop new approaches and test them out in turn. Such ongoing monitoring depth is very badly needed, if the relevance programme is to be developed as a positive educational experience for the pupils. (More so perhaps than with other subjects, since pupils may enter the relevance programme with preconceptions which militate against its effectiveness.) While a majority of teachers would as yet be ill equipped to undertake such research in a formal way, the findings could assist them in the interpretation of their daily experience and in moving towards more effective programmes. Such research would feed well into the deliberations of the Rudd model of inter-school consortia.

Induction of Supervisory and Advisory Staff. We come now to the induction of supervisory and advisory staff attached to regional or district education offices. This function has often been neglected or perfunctorily treated; and once again the seriousness of the omission has been described by Indian commentators. According to the Assessment Committee on Basic Education, the fundamental weakness in the implementation system for Basic schooling was the indifference of educational administrators to the scheme and their failure to institute effective measures of support in respect of matters such as the supply of materials for craftwork and disposal of craft products. The committee noted that in certain districts, where education officers had given Basic Education their full support, there had been praiseworthy results. In many instances, however, a chain of negativism passed from state capital to local education officers and to school principals. There is no easy solution to this problem. Design of induction courses that could transform the attitudes of these officers who have achieved some considerable status within the established system can never be easy. (See for instance Lallez 1974:68-9.)

There is no easy answer, but one mistake may be avoided. This is to assume that a cursory briefing on the relevance innovation is sufficient for senior educational personnel and that the main training effort should be concentrated on teaching staff. The reverse is indeed the case, for supervisory personnel, if attracted by the innovation, can provide teachers with support of many kinds including effective in-service training. One would suggest that supervisory and advisory staff should be given a lengthy induction course drawing upon the best insights and methods of management education. A live participatory role in programme development and evolution might assist also, provided that a spirit of dynamism is maintained.

As Lallez points out so convincingly, efficient programme development requires at least the concurrence of the regional supervisory staff. It might be wise, however, not to rely solely on this channel of communication. These officers have many other tasks and can easily assign a low priority to a relevance programme with which they have a little sympathy. Often, too, they include a substantial number of persons promoted direct from the schools on the basis of seniority (or political connections) who are ill equipped, in terms of education or experience, to give leadership in the process of educational innovation. Rogers and colleagues (1969), in a study of educational innovation in Thai schools, noted that far from giving leadership in this respect, the regional supervisory staff often learned of new educational practices from younger teachers who had been exposed to them at college.

The case for setting up some kind of parallel structure for the communication and support of the relevance programme and for the efficient transmission of feedback data from field to centre thus merits serious consideration. The structure might comprise some full-time staff and some teachers acting in a part-time capacity. The parallel staff would be inducted at some length into the relevance programme and would depend for their own status on the importance that they assign to it. Such staff might organise in-service training programmes, support joint course development projects, sponsor inter-school competitions or exhibitions, and above all visit schools to discover local problems and seek their solution.

A prerequisite for effective performance would be adequate transport facilities. Many Third World schools never see their district inspector or education officer from one year to another. Public transport in the rural areas is such that they confine their field visits to schools within easy reach. To support a practical innovative relevance programme the field staff should, however, have access to the schools. At the very least their travelling allowances for the use of public transport and where necessary modest rest-houses need to be adequate to cover their costs – around such details of procedure revolve the issues of success or failure.

The special position of regional (and central) staff already holding advisory posts in relevance topics such as agriculture, handicrafts and home science may be mentioned here. Such staff need to be given a clear position in the new scheme of things, whenever a relevance innovation is introduced, so that their efforts are directed towards promoting the innovation rather than discounting it. At the same time, it should be realised that they may find it difficult to think in innovative terms. The situation is again one demanding maximum attention rather than glossing over. A substantial induction programme leading on to a clearly defined role is surely called for.

Pre-service and In-service Teacher Trainers. Regarding the induction of pre-service and in-service teacher trainers, there is little documentary evidence to review. One forms a general impression that teacher training institutions have often failed to pay more than lip service to relevance programmes, that agriculture and craft instructors are accorded a lesser status than lecturers in academic subjects and that the equipment and materials needed for the study of practical subjects have often been lacking. Substantial, rather than cursory, induction programmes for training college principals, appointment of technically competent staff, and substantial induction of these and other teacher training staff into the new approach would seem to be required in pre-service training institutions along with a modest budget to purchase necessary requisites. Regarding in-service teacher trainers, the longest and most thoroughgoing induction programme was perhaps that at the Jeanes School, Kabete, in Kenya, during the 1920s and 1930s. Experienced teachers were given a two-year residential training in the techniques of pedagogy and in rural development topics, and were then assigned by their employers (usually mission stations) to upgrade the work of the schools in a particular area as itinerant teacher-educators. It is recorded, however, that they encountered difficulties, as practising teachers were sometimes better qualified than they and preferred to align their work to the priorities of the senior staff of the central mission school. The 'cultural missions' which travelled in Mexico in the 1920s and 1930s to give in-service teacher training built up their own corpus of experience. One question to which we return later is whether the concept of 'one-shot' in-service teacher training is in any case adequate. This normally provides an introduction to general concepts or, at best, an example of a relevance programme functioning in a situation possibly markedly different from what any particular teacher attending the course will face. An ongoing supportive programme would be preferable and then perhaps it would be better known by another name, with overtones of supporting teacher-led development projects rather than merely the teacher as the passive recipient of 'training'.

Pre-service Teacher Training. The training of new teachers in the relevance approach has in several instances been given a central place in the innovation strategy, though in other instances such training has been neglected. A key element in the Bakht er Ruda programme and in the Turkish rural education programme, teacher training for the rural environment, was also attempted in the Mexico of the later 1920s and 1930s (though with less success because of extensive migration of graduates to the towns). Conversion of teacher training schools to the Basic model and the founding of Basic training schools were accorded pride of place in the strategy to introduce Gandhian education also. A major constraint has been the difficulty of staffing the new group of training institutions with teachers competent in agriculture and in craft subjects. More recently the siting of curriculum development programmes in the Colleges of National Education (Tanzania) and in teacher training institutions at Yaoundé (Cameroon), Bunumbu (Sierra Leone) and elsewhere have illustrated a continuing awareness of this approach. The likely status-enhancing effects of these programmes have already been mentioned.

There is little information on the adequacy of these programmes in forming teacher skills and attitudes. A recurring problem, noted earlier, has been the loss of impetus when newly trained teachers are sent out to posts scattered throughout a school system in which many supervisors, school principals and teachers are opposed to change. This problem, and ways of minimising it, were touched upon in discussion of normative-re-educative strategies for innovation in Chapter 5 and are considered again later.

Induction of Principals. A vigorous induction of school principals into the relevance programme is one way of maximising the returns to pre-service (and in-service) training of teachers. The school principal who has become willing to assume management responsibility for a relevance programme in his school is only too pleased to encourage a newly trained teacher to use his skills in this area to the full. And unless the school principal *is* prepared to undertake this management role the prospects are bleak. The most vigorous pre-vocational studies programme in the schools of Sri Lanka are perceived to be those in which the principal takes the leadership role or actively supervises the programme or in which the pre-vocational studies teacher(s) stated that 'the principal gives me constant support'.

There is some documentation on two rather atypical programmes, each of which was relatively successful in terms of its own aims and objectives. At Bakht er Ruda, special accommodation had been provided, so that twenty to thirty headmasters and teachers could come into residence for two to three months at a time, learning about the latest handbooks and how to use them. Every headmaster and teacher would thus attend every five or six years and come to feel at home with the Bakht er Ruda staff, facilities and approach (Griffiths, 1975: 40). More recently, joint in-service induction of serving principals and teachers played a key role in the experimental programme at the Academy for Rural Development in Comilla.

The importance of this programme is that substantial results were obtained on the basis of a training programme directed primarily at village headmasters. The programme was ongoing in nature, included technical content, and was supported by 'management-by-objectives' style reportage of results obtained. On the other hand, the principals were not expected to transfer their newly acquired relevance orientation into school programmes singlehanded. The teachers designated as responsible for the clubs/interest groups (Sabuj Sangha activities) were trained at the academy also. (See Solaiman 1975: 10-11 for a detailed account.)

The circumstances at Comilla were, of course, exceptionally favourable. Village school headteachers were invited to participate in an action research project alongside the personnel of a prestigious national centre. It is illuminating nevertheless that these latter personnel, after close inspection of the local scene, decided that the headteacher was to be the key figure in this training programme, despite the requirement for an assistant teacher to be in day-to-day charge of Sangha affairs.

The importance of the induction process for school principals is widely acknowledged. The question is, how should this delicate task be accomplished, when the numbers of principals concerned is large. A first suggestion is that the induction process should be compulsory, of substantial duration and with a continuing element. Firmness is needed, if numbers prevent persuasiveness from playing its part. Principals may feel, on the basis of their accustomed lifestyle, that attendance at one briefing session is the most that should be required of them, and their school duties preclude anything more. (They may even feel that reading the first and last pages of a briefing document is more than sufficient!) The scope for creativity in developing innovation systems for inducting school principals is unlimited. Some combination of a substantial initial programme, preferably residential, and a continuing pressing involvement – perhaps in committee meetings at district level or in local curriculum development teams, might meet the need.

Induction of Serving Teachers. The induction of serving teachers, like pre-service training, has been accorded a key place in some programmes and a minor role in others. The cultural missions in Mexico were mentioned earlier. The first mission to Hidalgo comprised an educator, a soap-maker, a tanner, a physician, an agriculturalist and a teacher of folk songs. The second mission, to Morelos, had two agriculturalists, a carpenter, a home economics teacher and a pedagogue. Interest on the part of community members led to community education as the focus of the missions, along with methods of pedagogy, illustrated in the school of the town playing host to the in-service trainees. The first mission lasted three weeks but this was felt to be inadequate. By 1932 the schedule had been lengthened to four months, with the first ten weeks given over to preliminary work in the local community, prior to the arrival of teachers for their six-week in-service course. The number of teachers attending the course had by that date been limited to fifty, but there were as many as fourteen missions at work. A total of some two thousand teachers could thus be reached each year – a figure comprising not too unfavourably with the total number of federal rural schools of about seven thousand. An evaluation report in 1933 noted, however, that the six-week course was inadequate in view of the wide range of activities attempted, and that lack of local knowledge on the part of the 'missionaries' held back progress. Difficult local circumstances meant that permanent change could rarely be achieved. It was therefore decided to station the missions permanently at the Regional Peasant Schools, established in 1934 for agricultural and pre-service teacher training. This measure was short-lived, as President Cardenas's aides 'decided that the missions' principal role was to destroy provincialism and cultural barriers between classes and regions' (Ruiz 1963: 101). Despite these problems, the missions can be said to have played a key role in the Mexican programme, since they brought new ideas within the reach of innovative teachers, and constituted almost the only source of teacher induction (since graduates of pre-service rural teacher training courses tended to migrate to the towns).

The role of in-service training at Bakht er Ruda (complementary with handbook publication and pre-service training) and its role at Comilla (continuous training and contact with principals and teachers as the basis of the programme) have just been mentioned. In-service training of some kind has likewise been attempted in most instances where relevance programmes have been introduced on the basis of 'immediate (or speedy) universal adoption'. In such cases, however, the programmes have often been of a one-off character and often brief, lasting a matter of a few weeks. The best-documented programme, and one of the best organised, was that in Maharashtra, India, which ensured that each teacher entering the state-wide work-experience programme had attended an in-service training course lasting ten to fourteen days, including an introduction to the philosophy of work expereience, theoretical and practical studies in the work-experience topic and an introduction to the teachers' handbook. As noted earlier in this chapter some teachers felt that this substantial course of training was inadequate to prepare them to answer pupils' queries and cope with the practical side of the one-semester work-experience programme. This underlines a major problem of in-service training or induction courses. It takes a lot to make a teacher feel confident enough to *teach* a new subject, especially one with a practical dimension. To the thesis that the teacher should be seen to be exploring the subject along with the pupil, it may be answered that this exploratory approach is much facilitated when ample reference works are at hand (preferably in the local language), when modest funds are available to buy extra items, and when experts are at hand to give their advice. Such conditions are all too infrequent in Third World schools.

It would seem that problems of teacher confidence and competence are unlikely to be remedied by a minor increment in the duration of a one-shot course – from ten days to fifteen or even to twenty. The Maharashtra course of nearly two weeks full-time training compares favourably in duration with pupils' semester course of work-experience classes at no more than three periods a week. What is needed is perhaps help for the teacher in resolving problems as they arise. As a general principle, then, it would seem desirable to organise in-service programmes on a continuing basis, permitting the sharing of problems and the development of solutions, while maintaining teacher motivation and morale also.

Summary

Analysis of the innovation systems for generating and transmitting messages regarding the relevance innovations shows that these systems have typically been underdeveloped or neglected. There has been inadequate investment of human resources in research and development work at the centre and in the field, insufficient attention to the induction of the educators concerned at supervisory and school level with relevance work, and a lack of awareness of the need for these functions to be established on a continuing basis. These weaknesses evidently represent one important reason for the unsatisfactory outcome of many programmes. The need to attend to each link in the communications chain and to attend to work meticulously to ensure the effectiveness of each innovation system on the lines indicated by Bolam's model (1975) emerges clearly in the analysis presented in this chapter.

8 THE CLIENT SYSTEM: PUPILS AND THEIR FAMILIES

Thus far we have discussed two components of Bolam's model. It remains to discuss the impact of the innovation upon the client system, which includes educators, in their role as recipients of messages about the relevance programme, as well as pupils and the local community.

This chapter relates to pupils, their parents and other community members in their role as the final clients of the relevance innovation. Chapter 9 in turn considers educators as recipients of messages regarding the introduction of the innovation. This particular sequence has the merit of exposing the dismal circumstances in which teachers have often had to work – for the relevance innovation has time and again met with a hostile reception from the schools' users.

The Function of Schooling

We begin by considering the function of schooling as perceived by the citizens of the Third World. As noted earlier, policy-makers have often introduced the relevance innovation as a way of preparing young people to enter the 'traditional' sector of the economy, to remain as members of their home community and as participants alongside their parents in manual work and peasant agriculture. Pupils and their parents, however, have continued to see education as providing a ladder to prosperity, as an escape route from the subsistence economy. It is for this reason that they have been willing to make sacrifices to maintain their children in school. The first reaction to Western schooling in many countries was in fact one of hostility and suspicion. Later, as it became evident that children graduating from the early Western schools were given preference in appointments to government service or the private sector, the explosive demand for educational opportunities began. It still continues, each family hoping that one or more of its offspring will qualify for such employment. The alien institution has been accepted for its instrumental value. Families in the rural sector, at the mercy of drought, flood and other agricultural hazards, naturally value the opportunity to place one of their members in a job where income is regular and secure. The motivation has been further increased by the differential between earnings in the modern and traditional sectors. Educational qualifications provide the key to a new level of living (Blaug, Layard and Woodhall 1969, Psacharopolous 1973).

Foster's contention is that social status is closely correlated with income ranking, and hence with the educational qualifications which lead on to modern-sector jobs (Foster 1965:268-75). Educational qualifications apparently confer status on the family even when the young people concerned are unemployed or underemployed. Even resitting the school-leaving examination confers status. And it has recently been argued that there are definite psychic rewards (status, and hopes for the future) to continuing as a student rather than as an unemployed or underemployed youth: this may apply to the family as well as the student (Davis 1976).

Evidence from Africa indicates that there is a feeling of shame if a more educated child remains in the village unable to find a modern job. Several observers have documented parental insistence that school-leavers should go to the towns and seek some kind of paid employment. The pressure is greater on more educated youth (because of the chance of getting a better job). Heijnen (1968) indicated that the pressure was not too severe on local school-leavers who could spend a short time in town with relatives and then return home to cultivate a plot of cotton on their own, but was much more severe for school-leavers from areas where there was a shortage of good agricultural land.

Young people themselves profess to high occupational aspirations while they are in school and as yet have some hope of continuing their education further. A majority of middle-school pupils in Maharashtra and Sri Lanka, and of secondary school pupils in West Africa, for example, indicated their aspiration for professional level employment. It is true that pupils realise the odds against them. Their expectations are more humble – middle or lower-level modern-sector employment or no paid employment at all, as the case may be.[1] Yet they may keep their dreams until their student days are over. Few will wish to confess in advance that they are ready to forego the glamour, freedom and apparent affluence of urban life to labour beside their fathers and elder brothers in the fields.

The Status of Relevance Programmes

The high returns to a primary, middle or secondary-school leaving certificate have generated a negative response to work-experience programmes perceived as a threat to standards of attainment in these examinations. It is true that in the early stages of modernisation, parents reluctant to send their children for Western-style schooling urged on them by the government, often complained that the curriculum was irrelevant to village life. This phase was short-lived, however. Once rural parents faced the costs of sending their children to school (costs in terms of respectable clothing, stationery etc., and labour foregone, as well as sometimes transport costs and fees) they looked for equality of opportunity with children attending city schools. In India, for example, the 'ruralised' education programmes introduced from the late 1870s were discontinued in the second decade of the present century because villagers continually presented petitions asking for the same curriculum as urban schools, in order to have parity of prospects *vis-à-vis* government and related employment. One of the principal factors underlying the unpopularity of Gandhian Basic Education was the fact that it was not co-ordinated with orthodox educational structures, so that Basic school graduates sometimes had difficulty in gaining access to middle school and high school places and hence to the matriculation examination. The fact that the Basic curriculum omitted English, a language of value in the employment market and used at the time for matriculation and college studies, contributed to its unpopularity. The response of the rural population around Delhi illustrates the point:

> The Delhi administration took a policy decision around 1950 to convert all its schools located in the rural areas into the Basic pattern and to establish all the new schools to be opened in the villages as Basic schools. About five years later, when all the rural schools had already become of the Basic type, the policy had to be revised on account of the public pressure brought to bear on the authorities. It was argued that only the village children were treated with the fare of Basic education, while the city children continued to receive academic education which was supposed to give the latter an advantage over the former in the matter of receiving higher education and subsequently in the race for personal advancement. Incidentally this argument was supported by the fact that very few who had completed their education in a senior Basic school and sought admission into a higher secondary school succeeded in getting themselves admitted. (Salamatullah 1963.)

This dual system had not been intended, but the complex structure of schooling in India together with apathy and hostility towards Basic schools among educational administrators and secondary school headmasters led to a neglect of earlier recommendations for systematic transfer of able pupils from Basic schools to the high school stream at

11+ and 14+. And no powerful voice spoke for the conversion of private and municipal schools to the Basic model.

The lesson was well learned. The Indian Education Commission in 1966 proposed that work experience on a limited scale should be included as part of the regular school experience of every pupil. Duality was to be avoided. Apathy to the work-experience concept among educational administrators has again led to a slow and limited response, but in some states major programmes have been initiated, this time on a universal basis. Thus all pupils in Maharashtra are obliged to complete the work-experience courses prescribed for grades 8 and 9 as a pre-requisite for sitting the matriculation examination in grade 10. The timetable allocation is small (two or three periods a week). Hence there is no competitive advantage or disadvantage to any pupil arising in connection with this programme and public feelings have not been aroused. This degree of public acceptance should permit the quality of the programme to be raised steadily over the years, though in 1974 financial constraints were cited as limiting the possibilities for an activist approach to this end.

The Philippines community schools likewise encountered a great deal of public opposition, as parents objected to the children being taken from their classroom studies to do apparently uneducational work. 'The detrimental effect on the children who are made to labour during school hours make us jittery,' wrote one parent. 'I have even heard that there is a plan afoot . . . to clean the streets. An admirable and laudable act indeed! And favourable to *laissez-faire* municipal administration.' As noted earlier the digging of a fish-pond caused a similar reaction. 'Spare the children from the forced labour that the project will require,' parents requested. 'They ought not to spoil their clothes by being obliged to work in muddy places. Besides, why should they waste their precious study time that is not even enough to enable them to learn to read and write? Leave the swamp alone.' And at another school: 'Teachers were sensing that ominous signs were brewing . . . . Parents complained that their children were used as *camerinos* or street cleaners. The principal and some teachers were threatened to be manhandled and accused in court.' Parents at the latter school were persuaded to share the work of community improvement, while the teachers learned to correlate practical work and class studies. This latter achievement was rare, however, and the Director of Public Schools himself in 1956 confirmed parents' assertions that ordinary school work had suffered: 'We have wittingly or unwittingly done violence to accepted educational values and standards.'[2]

In Africa the 'adapted' curricula introduced in the 1920s were superficial in impact, with teachers and pupils alike regarding them as less important than the 'academic' subjects. In Kenya, school gardens were physically disrupted as symbols of an education system which kept Africans at the bottom of the economic ladder. Likewise, the school agriculture programmes introduced in Tanganyika in the 1950s were discontinued partly because they were perceived as irrelevant in view of the greater rewards of modern-sector appointments under Africanisation. The middle-school graduate could at that time earn more from a modest job in town than he could in the countryside, and the obstacles to setting up as a farmer in his own right were substantial. Resistance to the agricultural programmes on economic grounds – parents feared that the heavy time allocation for agricultural work would impair their children's academic progress – provided a solid base for the political opposition which overwhelmed this programme. Gardening and farmwork had become 'merely extra-curricular activities supervised by a few enthusiastic teachers in a small number of schools' (Morrison 1976:84-6). The self-reliance programme in contrast was founded on a sound political base, the Arusha Declaration of 1967, and applies to all students in the racially integrated education system of Tanzania. It has in consequence been more generally accepted. Nevertheless there is still some hesitation at this deviation from examination-oriented schooling. Parental comments similar to those cited for the Philippines have been reported, as have indications of parents allowing their children to absent themselves from school on self-reliance days.

Elsewhere in India the Upper Volta programme of Rural Education Centres foundered on this same issue. Parents welcomed the centres, hoping that they might be recognised later as primary schools. When their hopes were disappointed, they were unwilling to send their children to the centres. If the children stood no chance of gaining the primary-school leaving certificate then there seemed little point in sacrificing the contribution that they could make to the family's own labour-intensive agricultural efforts especially at peak seasons when every pair of hands was an asset. Under pressure from the authorities they would send younger children, whose labour power was less valuable (Ahmed and Coombs 1975:361).

Client response will always provide a severe test for the educational innovator. Educational reforms, including those relating to classroom method rather than structural change, remain a sensitive issue even in the more affluent countries. Much depends then upon tact and ability to see the clients' point of view – for if communications are poor and empathy is lacking, even a minor change can generate a negative response. A number of issues relating to the management of innovation may be elaborated briefly here.

First, *the degree of match or mismatch between the objectives of the policy-maker and those of school clients in respect of promotion within the education system and the structure of earnings differentials and status values in society* have been discussed already – access to higher levels of education and to modern-sector employment have typically been dependent upon results in a national school-leaving examination.

Secondly, it is important to establish *the degree of match between the new timetable incorporating the relevance innovation and clients' conception of the time needed for orthodox classroom studies*. Parents have had little to say about one or two periods a week of 'manual training' or 'health and hygiene' studies, where these have not been perceived to make major inroads on the time and energies of the pupils. Where manual work, social service etc. have been given the pre-eminent place in the timetable, however, then parents have felt dissatisfied. Consider, for example, the period of 'heavy farmwork' in the 1950s middle-school programme in Tanganyika, which accounted for about a third of the school year. Pupils were expected to labour in the fields from 6 am to 7.30 am and from 8 am to noon. After this, presumably fatigued, they were to have five periods of classroom studies (instead of their usual eight). The Basic school curriculum likewise focused on practical studies. The Zakir Husain Committee had suggested a time allocation of 3 hours and 20 minutes daily for craft (including agricultural) work out of a daily total of 5 hours and 30 minutes. Given the difficulties of introducing even a modest relevance component effectively, it would seem wise not to alienate public opinion by overgenerous allocation of time to compulsory practical work on a nationwide basis. The individual school may attempt more, but the principal would be wise again to reach an agreed position with the parents. It may be too that where a programme is well conceived and well led, interested pupils will put in extra time after school on a voluntary basis. This was certainly the case with some innovative pre-vocational studies programmes in Sri Lanka, and was one of the bases for the 'home projects' undertaken by pupils in the Philippines community and barrio high schools and in the Comilla district.

This leads thirdly to the question of arousing pupils' interest and motivation. Even where a programme runs somewhat counter to client priorities, it may still be viable, if pupils can be motivated. We may thus mention first the question of the effort to teach *interesting* (younger and older pupils) and *new income-yielding* (older pupils) skills; and to tap the reserves of *youthful idealism*. The Basic schools of contemporary Gujarat start their youngest pupils on various kinds of handwork suited to their age, then introduce them to the ginning, carding and spinning of cotton, using simple techniques. At this stage the pupils find these experiences intrinsically interesting. Older pupils again are introduced to Gandhian ideals. In the practical sphere they are taught a wide range of agricultural techniques and help cultivate a wide range of crops. As regards spinning, they spend a week or ten days working full-time at the *ambar charka*, which could in principle generate a substantial supplement to the poor family's budget (though in most instances, pupil interest would be sustained more through the direct return – the savings accruing from spinning for themselves the yarn needed for their next school uniform, or loyalty to Gandhi, or perhaps the escape from the routine of classroom studies!). There is no doubt, however, that in the period when Basic Education was being pursued as a matter of national policy, many schools fell far short of the range of equipment and facilities recommended by the Zakir Husain Committee and that the average teacher could not have sustained pupil interest for three hours a day. There is a strong possibility also that many teachers fell short on Gandhian idealism, and that pupils were instructed to undertake craftwork without any source of inspiration of the kind originally intended. Kale's hypothesis, on the basis of evidence from Maharashtra, that pupils take an especial interest in work-experience topics which are new to them rather than part and parcel of their everyday environment, may be mentioned here.

The interest of older pupils may thus be aroused through presentation of new and interesting activities, or if the activities undertaken seem likely to be of direct use to them, or through stimulating their sense of idealism. A combination of these factors is likely to be especially potent. Thus Lema (undated) noted, in a survey of self-reliance programmes, that pupil response was most enthusiastic where the ideals presented by President Nyerere had been interpreted through the introduction of pupils to new kinds of productive activity with some possibility of generating earnings after leaving school.

Although there is little documentation, one specific case has been noted in the literature. The initiation of post-school groups for Rural Education Centre graduates in Upper Volta by the rural education counsellor for Yatenga district seems to have led to improved morale among students and teachers in this district, as some continuing use could be seen for the studies undertaken. This raises the question of the *follow-up services provided for school-leavers*. Even where graduates of relevance programmes cannot be given their own parcel of land, some assistance in building a life in their home area may be possible. In Yatenga district, Rural Education Centre graduates have undertaken farming activities, have followed continuation learning programmes and correspondence courses to improve basic literacy, extend agricultural knowledge, acquire knowledge of book-keeping, and have diversified into fields such as commerce, handicrafts, transportation and agricultural repair work (Ahmed and Coombs 1975:351). As individuals, these young people could not have undertaken these initiatives. As a group, supported by the rural education counsellor and the rural development officer, they were able to develop a programme of activities suited to their local situation and interests.

The follow-up solution is by no means an easy one, however, and cannot be effectively implemented by decree. The kind of leadership which can see a way forward even in unpromising local circumstances is scarce. There is an additional problem: if too many schools encourage their ex-pupils to take up similar kinds of productive activity, the market may soon become saturated with their products. A cautious approach, based on government encouragement for seemingly promising initiatives, would seem to be in order here. Kwasi Boakye's proposal for experimental resource centres, where school pupils on day-release and ex-pupils also could be trained in agricultural and craft skills, would be one such approach, especially if supported by arrangements for ex-trainees to work on a co-operative basis or form post-school groups, on the lines developed in Upper Volta.

Pupil interest may also be aroused through the opportunity to share in the product of work-experience activities. The motivating forces of *student choice* (whether or not to participate and what to do) and of *provision for individual or small group projects* have been harnessed likewise in a few instances – notably in community service programmes (such as those undertaken by the Philippines community schools) and in gradualist or partial programmes (such as the Rajasthan earn-learn project, in which participation is voluntary) rather than in systemwide, highly structured programmes. The weekend 'hobby club' operating in Poona (Maharashtra) during the 'action research' phase of the work-experience programme showed what could be done where resource endowments were favourable and pupils could attend voluntarily to undertake their own projects. Such conditions are difficult to reproduce on a large scale. The balance of returns from compelling pupils to participate in rather narrow or stereotyped programmes and allowing rather fewer pupils the opportunity to participate in more differentiated activities should always be considered, however.

Finally, we come to the question of *the effort to explain and win public support for relevance programmes* and even to *silence dissent*. In some cases this has been neglected. In other cases, the programmes have been presented as part of the philosophy of a respected national leader, such as Gandhi or Nyerere. This does not necessarily ensure their acceptance. In other cases again, the programmes have been introduced as the solution to problems of rural deprivation or youth unemployment. The danger here is of disillusion when it is found that schools cannot solve these problems alone and, in many cases, fall short of a convincing effort to do so. In yet other instances, strong political pressures have served to enforce the programmes and perhaps to silence dissent. Such pressures serve to protect the programmes though not necessarily to make them more effective. Under these circumstances, a change of government or leadership may then lead to discontinuation.

Notes

1. For data on aspriations and expectations, see *inter alia* Foster (1965), Clignet and Foster (1966), Heijnen (1968), Gore *et al*. (1966), Kale (1973).
2. See Batten (1959:89-90, 155) and UNESCO (1955).

9 THE CLIENT OR USER SYSTEMS: EDUCATORS AND THEIR MOTIVATION

This consideration of the second group of clients of the innovation systems, the educators who have new responsibilities as recipients of a message connected with the relevance programmes, focuses primarily on the question of motivation. It commences with supervisory personnel such as schools inspectors and education advisers.

Supervisory Personnel

Lack of documentation is a handicap here. Often such persons have been expected to play an administrative and advisory role in respect of a relevance innovation, while lacking the necessary skills and expertise, as well as conviction regarding the merits of the innovation. They have further had little incentive to acquire the necessary skills or to regard the innovation with open-mindedness. The majority of such personnel have been aware rather that they would receive no special prospects of promotion or salary increments for their work in this field. There have been exceptions. In some cases, regional education staff have been personally convinced of the importance of some part of a relevance programme and have pursued it in the spirit of idealism. There have also been instances where a regional or district education officer, having an above-average competence in this sphere, has pursued a government-sponsored relevance programme with vigour, believing that he can shine sufficiently, relative to his fellows, to gain a national reputation in this field and hence a promotion. In general, however, the task of devising incentive systems that might generate a positive motivation of schools inspectors or education advisers towards vigorous support of relevance programmes has been neglected. The very difficulty of devising such an incentive scheme has contributed to this neglect. The possibility of setting up a parallel system of advisory officers, committed on a full-time basis to the support of the relevance innovation (and hence deriving their personal status from the importance which they and others attach to the innovation) merits consideration as an alternative or supplementary approach.

Principals and Teachers

Recent years have seen the beginnings of serious reasearch into the factors which influence the response of principals and teachers in the West in educational innovations. The limited take-up of non-compulsory innovations, such as the courses prepared by curriculum development teams or audiovisual aids, has contributed to interest in this field. Increased governmental involvement in the details of educational reform has contributed also. Management problems in the large complex organisation which some schools have become have also been analysed (Gross, Giaquinta and Bernstein 1971).

The study by Gross, Giaquinta and Bernstein raises the type of issues that are perceived as determinants of successful implementation of educational innovation. The unsuccessful attempts to introduce 'activity methods' to teachers at Cambire was unsuccessful for reasons more complex than teacher resistance: the interaction between new teaching methods introduced to teachers in abstract form; the requirements for new knowledge and skills; new materials; new organisational structures, conflicted with ingrained teacher habits.

A changeover to the new pedagogy would require substantial new learnings by teachers and pupils and could not be introduced by ultimatum. The teachers were, moreover, uncertain about the consequences of the innovation for their futures, suspecting (correctly) that they might be transferred to other schools if the superintendent was dissatisfied with their response.

How often has the 'relevance' innovation been introduced in the form of generalised 'objectives' or philosophy, to teachers working in overcrowded premises, hard-pressed to obtain even the chalk they need for chalk-and-talk? How often have teachers been expected to introduce activities related to the world of work and community service or community life, without guidelines, reference materials or funds to purchase equipment and materials for practical work – aware too that the local school inspector, who signs the recommendation for the annual salary increments, believes in good old-fashioned teaching and nothing else! Under such circumstances, there is little incentive to press on with the innovation. Rather, there is the temptation to play it down on the excuse that the necessary resources – equipment, teacher skills – are not available.

The Structure of Incentives

The structure of the incentives and disincentives facing principals and teachers may be considered more formally under the following headings:

career incentives and disincentives (promotions, increments and tranfers)

- concordance/discordance with personal characteristics, values and interests
- perception of the innovation by pupils and their families
- material support
- adequacy of induction and training
- professional recognition and companionship.

Career Incentives and Disincentives (Promotions, Increments and Transfers)

An educator who has completed his professional training and established himself in his career has a vested interest in the status quo. The teacher has his lessons prepared, the principal has a rule of thumb for making adjustments to the school timetable. There is a natural inertia in the system. This inertia might be lessened if teachers could see a positive return for themselves to the efforts required to gain mastery of a new range of educational activities. Often, however, the structure of incentives has been negative. In particular, the relevance innovation has been transmitted to the schools through school inspectors or advisers who are unconvinced of its merits or take no interest in it. These officials have a major say in the important matter of salary increments, transfers and promotions. These matters assume great importance in the closed world of a rural education district – where the supervisor is in a position of power and authority. Many teachers in rural areas live in hope of a transfer to a more congenial post – to an assignment in the towns with their modern facilities or to the teacher's home area. Sometimes teachers have been posted to the rural areas as a 'punishment transfer' (e.g. for having supported the wrong political party) or because new teachers have to accept a first posting there. Perhaps they are separated from their families. In these circumstances, cultivation of a good relationship with the supervisory officer is the paramount consideration. There is no easy solution to these problems. One possibility in theory would be to require a report from a relevance supervisory or advisory officer as well as the regular officer before deciding upon promotions, increments and transfers. This system would probably be very difficult to operate in practice, given the entrenched behaviour patterns in educational administration.

It is difficult to manipulate the structure of incentives to generate positive attitudes towards relevance programmes among the teaching force as a whole. It is less difficult, however, to devise incentive structures that may provide a stimulus for teachers with an especial interest or talent in this field. An example from Sri Lanka may be cited here.

In 1974 it was decided that four outstanding principals of rural schools or schools in deprived urban areas should be accorded promotion to the highest salary scale for primary school principals, the scale applicable to the principal of Royal College Junior School in Colombo. At least one of these awards went to a headmaster who had shown great ability and application in developing the pre-vocational studies programme. An important feature of this scheme was the possibility of offering encouragement to innovative principals without removing them from their posts by promotion and thereby disrupting the creative work on which they were engaged.

Concordance/Discordance With Personal Values and Interests; Relation to Other Personal Characteristics such as Adaptability and Attitude to Teaching and to Personal Circumstances such as Travelling Times

A rewarding school visit in Sri Lanka was to a small, isolated village school. The children at this school were from impoverished labouring families and few stayed at school beyond the age of thirteen. They had nevertheless prepared a wonderful array of woodcarvings and had performed various other practical activities related to forest products. The headmaster was the son of a carpenter, had done woodwork as a hobby at school and training college, and continued with his interest in later life. The pre-vocational studies programme offered the opportunity to put his personal interests and abilities to the service of the boys in his school. His values generally led him to encourage his wife, also a teacher at the school, to develop an innovative programme in fibrework for the girls. His personal circumstances – living in a principal's cottage adjacent to the school – facilitated programme development. If schoolwork intruded a little on his leisure time this was perhaps as much of a blessing as a burden, given the isolated position of the school. Often, circumstances are the reverse. A city-bred teacher has little knowledge of the countryside, of practical agriculture or the traditional uses of local resources. He identifies with the world of the book, of traditional school subjects and examinations. He lives in an urban area and spends long hours commuting to and from the school each day. Or he takes lodgings in a 'backward' area and devotes his time and energies to obtaining a transfer to a more congenial environment.

A degree of idealism and commitment to the philosophy of relevant education is equally important. Consider, for example, the case of Sri Bahu Bhai Shah, founder of the Basic school in Gujarat, who resigned from his post with the Inland Revenue to follow in the steps of

Gandhi. He set up his base in an unpromising rural area, took responsibility for a number of primary schools in the area, set up a post-Basic secondary school and initiated extension and other programmes. Other Gandhian educators and numerous educators the Third World over have felt moved by the same ideals – to devote their lives to the uplift of impoverished rural communities through relevant education and associated activities.

Perception (Favourable/Unfavourable) of the Innovation by Pupils and their Families

Another potent factor controlling teacher motivation is the attitude of the schools' clients to the relevance innovation. If teachers in a rural area are subjected to continuing pressure from parents to devalue a relevance programme, they will feel substantially discouraged, especially since they are unlikely to be under much direct pressure from supervisory education personnel (who visit the schools but rarely) to counteract this influence.

Material Support

Another major cause of inertia has been lack of necessary resources. The fact that many schools, even in rural areas, lack sufficient agricultural land to support a work-experience programme, has already been elaborated. Many schools likewise suffer from severe financial problems. Hence the introduction of a relevance programme often means the staff purchasing materials from their own meagre salaries, or fund-raising among the local community. This strategy is, however, ineffectual among the less affluent sections of society, and the more ineffectual where parents feel, as they often do, that work experience and similar programmes are a waste of precious school time and a misuse of teacher skills.

Adequacy of Induction and Training

In general, the induction and training has been inadequate, and a structure of continuing support absent. It is arguable, indeed, that schools' modest response to relevance innovations has often originated in lack of understanding on the part of school principals as to how they should amend school timetables, assign relevance work to their staff, and to a lack of confidence on the part of the teachers that they can handle this new material.

Professional Recognition and Companionship

The importance of this kind of motivation is obvious, both on *a priori* grounds and from the literature on educational innovation generally. There is little direct evidence, however, in connection with relevance programmes, since information pertaining to this topic has rarely been recorded, but professional support has assisted the implementation of several programmes: the Philippines community school movement grew to nationwide dimensions and was sustained over a period of years through the agency of the Association of Philippine School Superintendents and its annual seminars; Fuggles-Couchman believed inter-school agricultural competitions to be a potent stimulus in the development of vigorous school agriculture programmes in the Tanganyika of the 1950s; and inter-school competitions were used to good effect at Comilla.

We have reviewed six areas where a relevance innovation needs to concord with the interest of a multi-faceted and vitally interested group of clients, the educators. The discussion simply underlines again our frequent observation that introducing innovation into schools is not simply a matter of good intentions and bright ideas. It is an enterprise demanding broadminded and skilful political management.

Part Four
CONCLUSION AND POLICY IMPLICATIONS

10 APPROACHES TO EDUCATIONAL RELEVANCE IN THIRD WORLD SCHOOLS

What emerges for policy from this review? First, the need for greater clarity regarding aims and objectives or programme rationale. Second, some fairly strong conclusions regarding the alternatives in respect of innovation strategy. Third, a statement of priorities for international agencies wishing to support moves towards more relevant schooling in the Third World.

Programme Rationale

Past experience indicates that relevance programmes for school-going children are *not* an appropriate vehicle for the rectification of social and economic ills. This conclusion rests in part upon the difficulty of conveying the necessary skills and motivation to the thousands of teachers in a nation's schools. It rests in part upon the fact that school-going children are not well placed to influence their elders in a traditional, or in any, society. It rests, finally, upon the observation that the amelioration of problems such as rural poverty and disease, or school-leaver discontent, cannot be solved by unilateral action within the education sector. Multi-agency programmes would be required to provide for changes such as land reform, provision of irrigation water and channels, provision of agricultural extension and other services, development of rural credit and co-operative societies, provision of drinking water and health services, and other infrastructural amenities. Without such programmes the schools alone can normally accomplish little. If, on the other hand, such multi-faceted programmes have been instituted, the contribution made by explaining them to schoolchildren, or involving such children in related activities, is likely to be a minor, though positive one.

It does not follow from these generalisations that *no* school can make a useful contribution to development in its environment. Under outstanding leadership such a contribution is possible. Nevertheless, such a contribution typically involves extension and counselling work with ex-pupils and/or adults as well as the relevance programmes for schoolchildren. Work in school then becomes preparatory to participation in further sponsored activities after leaving school.

The best rationale for in-school relevance programmes would thus seem to be the direct affirmation that a curriculum which includes these programmes is more balanced than one which does not. In other words, work activities, and health-related or community-related studies or projects are best justified in the same fashion as history, arithmetic and religion; they *have something worthwhile to contribute to the process of education*. A well-conducted relevance programme is thus assumed on an *a priori* basis to benefit pupils as much as, or to be desirable as a complement to, more orthodox school studies. A further justification might be the *a priori* belief that a well-conducted relevance programme should make a small, positive contribution to the solution of social and economic problems, either immediately or over the longer term – a belief again held on intuitive grounds, in the knowledge that no direct measurement of this contribution might ever be possible.

Given these *a priori* assumptions regarding the benefits of a well-conducted relevance programme, the question then becomes one of practicalities. Are the schools *in fact* able to offer imaginative or competent programmes in this field? The answer emerging from the present study is that some schools are so able. Where system-wide reform has been attempted, there has typically been a substantial 'tail' of schools which have been unsuccessful.

Alternative Strategies

These observations lead on to a consideration of alternative strategies. Are there certain strategies by means of which high quality relevance programmes can be ensured? The evidence of the present study suggests that a partial or stepwise programme, vigorously pursued, might lead to high-quality programmes in most participating institutions. Among the possible strategies offered for consideration here, the first is thus the stepwise development of a subpopulation of innovating institutions. This would be the preferred policy, if political and other pressures allowed such a choice. The second model offered for consideration is that of universal adoption of a relevance orientation but with a two-tier system permitting stepwise development of high-quality programmes in an expanding group of selected innovative schools. This policy would have much to commend it where political pressures necessitated immediate system-wide adoption of some kind of relevance venture. A third strategy involves the omission of any special relevance programme but the attempt to reorient the existing curriculum towards activity methods and local relevance. An attempt to build on its strengths and overcome its weaknesses would be appropriate where the government was unwilling to provide the resources and organisational infrastructure for a major relevance programme. These three strategies would seem, on the basis of the analysis presented in this study, to have substantial credibility. They represent, of course, a selection from a wider range of possibilities, a selection based on a composite view of the educational situations prevailing in Third World countries in general.

Strategy 1. Stepwise Approach Through a Special Institutional Development Programme for Education Relevance and Quality

The stepwise approach has emerged from the preceding chapters as offering, in principle, the opportunity to develop high-quality relevance programmes without the problem of a tail of badly performing schools.

The term 'special institutional development programme' should not be taken to imply the creation of large, expensively equipped institutions. In fact, the opposite is intended. Some of the most relevant programmes may be found in the smallest village schools. Relevance programmes may in fact be especially difficult to organise in large multi-stream schools with their bureaucratic structures and with expensive facilities often tailored to curricula imported from the developed countries. 'Institutional development' refers in this section to a process focused on the staff of selected schools and also to the creation of new kinds of educational institutions such as 'consortia' of teachers from small groups of neighbouring schools or 'resource centres' staffed by small groups of craftpersons and agriculturalists.

Strategy for Change. The stepwise approach suggested here relies primarily upon what Chin termed the *normative-re-educative* strategy for change rather than the use of the government's legal powers or the mere dissemination of persuasive arguments. The lessons of this study would seem to be that programme quality requires understanding, competence and personal commitment on the part of the educators concerned; and that educators cannot be coerced into manifesting theses characteristics. Rather, such characteristics emerge as the fruit of a long period of intense involvement with the reform in question, permitting internalisation of the norm as well as the development of the competence and confidence required for educators to give it practical expression in the course of their daily work. Personal commitment is here assumed to arise from close and prolonged co-operation with relevance specialists, in a relevance-oriented institutional framework – a 'pilot' or 'innovative' school. Competence is assumed to require access to specialised information and help in transforming it into knowledge, skills and teaching-learning techniques for daily use with pupils. A substantial research and development effort is assumed to be necessary to transform the relevance concept into such detailed specifications, some being of general applicability and some relating to particular local circumstances. In the stepwise model much of this research and development work would take place within the network of innovatory schools, backed up by persons with special expertise in programme development or relevance skills. Under these conditions, general principles and local adaptations and variations could be evolved, while teachers in participating institutions would tend to identify with the relevance concept and would gain the understanding, competence and commitment required for effective implementation. Such teachers would finally constitute a pool to be drawn upon for assisting with induction, supervisory and development work and for taking a leadership role in programme expansion.

It may be noted that the interpretation of the *normative-re-educative* approach adopted here is itself an innovation. Teacher-centred approaches in the past have leaned more towards pre-service and in-service teacher training programmes. The weakness of such programmes has been that intensive training has been followed by the dispersal of trainees into an often unreceptive environment, with little follow-up of their relevance training. Under such conditions, only exceptional trainees could utilise their learnings to the full and maintain a positive attitude to the reform programme. The institutional development approach, in contrast, would provide for the training of school principal and staff as a team by the support personnel. In other words, all efforts towards relevance, by the support personnel and by individual school staff, would be made in a favourable institutional climate and might therefore be expected to bring maximum returns. This is not to say that a teacher training college focused on relevance activities would be undesirable or that no effort should be made to induct pre-service teacher trainees into the relevance concept. Such efforts could be dangerous, however, especially in the early stage of the programme. Each country has an established tradition of teacher training and such institutions have a natural tendency to behavioural inertia. Unless this could be circumvented by creating special machinery to encourage innovation, it might perhaps be best to rely on the school-based development programme initially, and to make arrangements to familiarise new teachers with the work of a number of innovatory schools. Personnel from these schools might later be deputed to organise college programme or courses in the relevance field.

The Relevance Innovation. It may be noted that with a manageable number of independently innovating institutions, flexibility should be as attainable as it is desirable. It would be possible to begin with any age group that seemed appropriate, and to extend the coverage as desired, from kindergarten to junior secondary, from ex-pupils who have just concluded their full-time studies to older members of the community. This flexibility would permit each school to build on its own strengths. A woman teacher with a full crafts training in basket-weaving or lacework might take junior secondary girls through the craft, give advanced tuition to ex-pupils and help them with developing market outlets. Such a programme would not make sense on a national scale, because of market limitations, nor would most schools have a teacher with the necessary skills. Other schools might have other strengths, however, and develop quite different ventures, some with adults, some with recent leavers, some with older pupils and some with the youngest pupils in the schools.

Flexibility in choice of subject matter is equally essential. It means that a school with plenty of good agricultural land would be free to respond fully and creatively to the potential for agricultural development in the area. A neighbouring school with a quarter acre of cultivable land and a large number of pupils, would be free likewise to seek its relevance in some other sphere, (perhaps also arranging for older pupils or ex-pupils to benefit from the facilities of the first school if they so wished). Flexibility also permits adjustment to the seasons – with craftwork or community studies and community service being fitted into the agricultural slack seasons.

A further desirable feature of the stepwise model is the possibility of attending carefully to the development of suitable principles of procedure. The way a relevance programme is presented to pupils may be a key factor in determining whether or not the programme yields positive benefits as an educational experience which engages pupils' attention in constructive fashion and through contributing in a small way over the years to the build-up of constructive attitudes in society at large. Some effort was made earlier to identify certain broad principles of procedure that might be adopted. Much more detailed work is required, however, if principles of procedure are to be evolved which make sense in the school situation. This work should be possible at the level of an 'innovating' institution supported by a curriculum specialist. Stenhouse's (1975) discussion of his own steps towards identifying principles of procedure in the humanities field provides a useful heuristic model.

Innovation Systems: Communications and Induction. The structure of communications and provision for induction, should represent a much lesser problem under the model proposed here than in a model in which 'immediate universal adoption' is attempted. The machinery for communications would be able to grow organically, with regular meetings and exchange of written materials as the main vehicle of communications between participating educators, and with publications and occasional seminars at innovating schools to disseminate the work in hand to educators at large. Relationships between innovating institutions and nearby schools could likewise be built up on an *ad hoc* or organic basis, according to teachers' special interests, when the time was felt to be ripe.

The induction process would comprise mainly the extension of the relevance programme to cover more schools. This could likewise be undertaken at a pace which would not damage programme quality or stifle creativity. It may be suggested here that schools entering the programme during the early stages of the expansion process should not be selected on the basis of status – large enrolments and 'important' principals. Rather, school principals who had developed the relevance approach on a voluntary basis, or principals and teachers who had joined in the work of neighbouring innovatory institutions, would be the natural candidates to lead a new programme. Evidence of the existence of an enthusiastic group of teachers, including notably the school principal (plus evidence that they had some basic understanding of the relevance approach and some creative ideas on how to develop it in the context of their own school), should be the key criteria in the admission of a new school to the recognised relevance network.

Motivation of the Schools' Clients. Within this model, the problem of dualism would still exist (some schools following one pattern, some another). The problem should be manageable, however. The vital point would be to ensure that parents viewed the entry of their children's school into the 'innovatory' category as a privilege rather than a hardship. To this end parents would need to be consulted or at least kept well informed about the programme from the first. There should further be no massive or sudden disruption of the school's programme of studies. New activities and approaches might be introduced gradually, as teachers acquired the necessary knowledge and skills or tried out new approaches. Some activities might initially be introduced on a voluntary basis in after-school hours. Indeed, the use of out-of-school hours for time-consuming activities might be considered (staff being paid accordingly), even where all pupils were involved, so that pupils would have the same time for orthodox studies as children at other schools. Parents might thus come to feel that their children were getting 'extra' tuition and not less than children elsewhere and might well not grudge the additional opportunity cost of foregoing their children's labour.

If promotion from grade to grade or selection from one level of schooling to the next or eligibility for good jobs depends on achievements in externally set and marked examinations, the place of the innovation will need to be weighed delicately.

Where the aim is to transform the curriculum as a whole, then the policy of introducing new activities in addition to the old curriculum is not tenable beyond the first term or so. Where the reform affects examination (or immediately pre-examination) grades, an appropriate strategy might be to prepare separate versions of the school-leaving examination papers for pupils at the innovating schools, with a guarantee that the pass rate would not be less than, and might be higher than, that for the more traditional papers or than school results in previous years.

Another strategy which would merit the most careful consideration, would be to provide extra tuition in the 'difficult' examination subjects, as a compensation for involving pupils in an innovatory relevance programme. Certain examination subjects are sometimes considered easy, as there is a high pass rate. Other subjects, such as mathematics or a second language, may be considered difficult, if pass rates or marks for some reason are set much lower. Provision for small group tuition in difficult subjects, would help parents perceive the innovating institution as offering educational quality all round ('extra' in fact), rather than seemingly diverting children's efforts from their academic studies towards irrelevant relevance activities!

Educator Motivation. Educator motivation should be much less of a problem in the stepwise model than in system-wide schemes. In the first place, there would not be the same problem of communicating with every school through a reluctant hierarchy of district supervisors. True, education inspectors and other administrators would need to be given the most favourable possible view of the innovation, through participation in innovatory activities or at least regular acquaintance with them. Otherwise they might well make difficulties. They need not be key links in the motivational chain from programme initiators to programme implementers, however. The latter, school principals and teachers, should not present a severe problem as regards motivation, since they would have been selected as natural innovators or as persons with an interest in new approaches.

The question of cash incentives and disincentives should not be neglected, however. At the very least, travelling costs incurred in connection with the relevance programme should be met, and preferably an allowance or some salary increments paid to compensate for time and effort devoted to development work, after school activities, etc. The possibility of establishing a special cadre of innovatory personnel, paid on a higher salary scale and posted separately so that their skills are not wasted in non-innovatory situations, might also be considered.

The motivation of teachers in innovatory schools could be sustained by their regular contact with a curriculum or relevance specialist, anxious to report favourably on their progress in a national newsletter and to his colleagues; and perhaps by inter-teacher recognition and companionship, if a group of neighbouring innovative schools were to work together on the lines suggested by Rudd (1973).

Three final points may be made before leaving this model. One concerns the geographical distribution of innovatory schools. The initial batch of schools should cover the different agro-climatic zones etc. of the country but should be reasonably accessible to ensure adequate support. Schools selected for subsequent admission to the scheme ought not, however to be dispersed at large distances from these schools. Rather it might be desirable to build up 'consortia' of innovating schools within reach of each original innovating school (Hagerstrand 1965). Venturing to new areas might perhaps be left until there was a sufficient cadre of committed and experienced educators to cover a further geographical dispersion without difficulty.

A second point concerns provision for ex-pupils. It would seem wasteful to introduce a relevance programme for school-going pupils and then to make no provision for interested ex-pupils to follow up their earlier work. The appointment of a teacher as co-ordinator or counsellor for ex-pupils' activities, with a reduced teaching load or a special allowance, may be considered here. Alternatively, a special counsellor might be appointed to service school-leaver programmes at several adjacent schools. Provision of a small budget to cover tuition and guidance from craftsmen and others would also facilitate progress on this score. The school-leaver programme need not be aligned only to productive activities. Cultural, social service or sports activities (and even assisting with school activities, e.g. kindergarten classes) might also be relevant, helping young people relate to life in their home communities at the critical stage when the support of the school is withdrawn.

A third point concerns *special ventures* which might be launched alongside the innovatory school-based programmes just described. One such venture might be the systematic exploration of the use of local resources and low-cost appropriate technology in connection with work experience or other programmes.

Another venture might be the development of a limited number of resource centres, bringing together craftsmen and perhaps agriculturalists to provide for the part-time tuition of school-going pupils and part-time or full-time tuition of school-leavers; and also providing counselling and support for the latter as they attempt to set themselves up in self-employment or co-operative employment.

Another such venture might be the initiation of teacher-led research, on the model proposed by Stenhouse (1975), with teachers conducting systematic research into their own relevance programmes. As noted previously, only some teachers would have the necessary background to do this, but such efforts as might be feasible could well bring great benefits to the schools in general. In particular, some insights might be gained into effective principles of procedure.

Strategy 2. Compulsory (Speedy) Universal Adoption With a Stepwise Component

Of the three strategies discussed here, compulsory and immediate (or speedy) universal adoption of the relevance innovation is perhaps the least attractive viewed from a management perspective. The chief disadvantage of this approach is the persistent problem of the long tail of schools with inadequate or unimpressive programmes. Governments have repeatedly felt drawn to the system-wide approach, however, in the belief that schools could make a substantial impact on intractable social and economic problems. In some cases, there has been a genuine belief or hope that effective, high-quality programmes could be launched in *all* schools straight away. In other cases, policy-makers have been well aware of the problems of the tail, but for administrative reasons or from fear of public hostility to any form of dualism (some schools introducing relevance programmes while others are exempt) have gone ahead with universal adoption nevertheless. It cannot be overemphasised in this connection that *even though there may be immediate universal adoption in theory, there is always gradual or partial adoption in practice.* Some schools, often many, lack the means (human skills and non-human resources) and some the will for immediate effective action.

These schools comprise the tail.

In the case in which the central authorities commit themselves to a compulsory universal programme what can the educational administrator do to optimise levels of performance?

His first step might be to argue the case for a two-tier approach to the innovation. A two-tier system would incorporate a modest definition of the relevance activities for system-wide implementation, together with a commitment to more thoroughgoing reform in an expanding network of 'pilot' or 'innovative' schools. In other words, Strategy 1. could be applied, with appropriate modifications, for intensive programme development. At the same time, an adequate system of induction, training and motivation would be required for the system-wide reform.

Suppose further that, as seems likely, the high-level policy-makers were to express dissatisfaction with the idea of a two-tier system, if this meant that intensive relevance programmes were to be introduced initially in only a score or so of schools. What would be the position of the educational administrator in this situation? He might then argue for a massive infusion of resources, especially skilled human resources, into the innovation system, sufficient to support a network of innovatory schools in each district or region, and schemes for linking other schools to innovatory schools in local programme 'consortia'. He might argue, for example, that if twenty per cent of the timetable is to be given over to relevance work, then a relevance development and supervisory staff complement would be required, roughly equal in size to the entire normal complement of such staff – the argument being that the latter operate within a long-established tradition. This extra staff complement would not only provide for research and development personnel but would permit the establishment of an advisory-supervisory superstructure for relevance studies running parallel to the normal supervisory hierarchy. In this way, the barriers to effective action imposed by the inertia or negative attitudes of the schools inspectorate could be avoided. Communications and support services would be mediated instead by officers whose sole claim to importance would be the relevance innovation, who would have had a substantial induction into this programme and who might therefore be expected to offer significant leadership in programme development.

Another difference from the stepwise model would be the fact that, with all schools required to develop relevance programmes of at least a modest kind, it might prove possible to identify a higher proportion of the natural innovators, of the pool of talent in this sphere latent among the teaching force. Identification of these natural innovators and integration of these schools into the intensive institutional development programme would provide for a wider span of creative endeavour as well as assisting in the process of effective expansion.

Regarding client reaction, the best strategy would again seem to be to avoid antagonising pupils and their families; by providing for consultation and explanation, avoidance of excessive inroads into the time available for classroom studies, exemption of examination year pupils, and giving the new programme intrinsic interest through careful choice of subject matter and attention to principles of procedure. The attempt to induce willing client participation by including relevance studies in national school-leaving examinations seems undesirable, however. Though it might seem to stimulate parental pressure on the school in the short term (pressure to make sure adequate attention is given to this sphere), it might tend in the longer term to increase public opposition to the programme at the national level, due to the evident discrepancies in programme functioning between one school and another, and between pupils who can afford to purchase equipment and materials and those who cannot. From the educational viewpoint there is also the extremely deleterious backwash effect of examinations on what is intended to be a creative and flexible exploration of the life and work of the community. An arrangement such as that adopted in Maharashtra might be a useful compromise in certain circumstances. The school principal in Maharashtra has to put his or her name to a statement that a pupil has completed the required programme of work experience (in grades 8 and 9) before the pupil is accepted as a candidate for the matriculation examination (in grade 10). No work-experience programme is prescribed for the matriculation year, though pupils may fill in any gaps in their work-experience programme during this period. This arrangement enables the principal to resist parental pressure against the programme if he wishes to do so. It does not, of course, prevent the principal from tolerating or encouraging neglect of the programme, if he himself so prefers. Remedies for the latter ill would include better induction of principals and perhaps arrangements to evaluate school performance, the results reflecting on the efforts of the school principal, rather than the performance of individual pupils.

Strategy 3. Retention of the Orthodox Curriculum but With an Effort to Introduce Pupil Activities and Greater Local Relevance

Some countries have been reluctant to launch programmes of work experience or community-related schooling – perhaps because of educators' memories of unsuccessful colonial schemes or from a desire to remain close to the internationally accepted pattern of schooling. It does not follow that relevance is entirely neglected in such countries, however. Indeed, they may sometimes be following a strategy which has certain real advantages. This is to attempt to move towards local relevance within the structure of the existing school subjects. A great strength of this approach is its compatability with the work of innovative educators in the 'more developed' countries, where so many Third World educational administrators and teachers attend advanced courses or make study tours; and around which the international literature of educational research and development largely revolves. Progressive educators have for some decades laid stress on making the school curriculum more relevant to the child and, especially at primary school level, introducing the principle of pupil activity. In so far as a nation attempts to build up a cadre of educators well versed in current world educational thinking, it is therefore tending to build up a climate of opinion favourable to the activity approach and to curriculum development requiring inquiry and local observation by the pupils. And in so far as a nation sets up a large curriculum development programme with persons trained in this way it is likewise tending to move the education system towards relevance. The strength which such a generalised programme might acquire through being rooted in the dynamic of international educational thought could be very considerable. University educators, government curriculum development personnel, and leading citizens generally, would rest secure in the knowledge that they were part of the wider international community.

Despite these advantages, Strategy 3. could have severe limitations as an approach to relevance. At the curriculum development level, there might be a tendency for the centre of gravity of new curricula to remain where it has always been – around a list of scientific concepts and phenomena, a list of historical and geographical facts and principles, or whatever, that no one (or no committee!) would be willing to drop. Hence there might be a tendency for local relevance and pupil activities to be introduced either in a very nominal way (by including the life cycles of a key crop and of the mosquito in the biology curriculum, and so on) or added on (as in excursions to collect specimens or to visit the local market). It is difficult for a subject specialist to view his subject 'backwards', beginning from the local scene, and selecting concepts for study on the basis of essentially local priorities. This posture has been adopted in some instances. It may be easier psychologically and intellectually to achieve such a reversal of stance in some subjects than others, in social studies rather than science, for example, or in biological science rather than in physical science perhaps. For some reason also the concept of devising low-cost approaches to the teaching of handicrafts, science etc. has made limited impact. Perhaps this again reflects a pattern of interests derived from the international scene (from machine-centred societies with man-made environments where anything from nature is a scarce resource!).

Conservative thinking is likely to be a serious problem at classroom level also. Teachers are likely to continue viewing the school subjects as being focused on the same subject matter that they themselves studied when at school or college. They may have difficulty in accepting a different conception of the subjects they teach and difficulty also in acquiring a confident understanding of new subject matter. The introduction of the activity approach likewise may be retarded by teachers' difficulties in understanding what is required and why (as well as by lack of an adequate resource base – materials, equipment and space to move about). Pupils and their families may likewise react against a change of approach. Client resistance should in principal be minimised under this strategy as there is no change in the names and time allocation of the various subjects on the timetable and no gross change in examination structures. In practice parents may raise substantial objections. The new relevant social studies curriculum introduced in Sri Lanka over the years 1972 to 1975, for example, elicited a surprising amount of opposition on the grounds that pupils were not on an equal footing in respect of the preparation of illustrated workbooks. 'Modern maths' likewise has also provoked client resistance throughout the world.

In a system-wide scheme, supervisors, principals and teachers lack motivation to implement changes in approach and may well raise objections through teachers' unions or alternatively ignore the reforms. The case for a stepwise strategy might therefore be considered. The reform would then become a special case of Strategy 1. above.

International Support

In some circumstances, the educator may have some freedom of choice regarding which of these three strategies, or which other general strategies, should be adopted. Political circumstances will often determine the nature and pace of any move towards relevance, however. The educator may still have some freedom of manoeuvre, however, regarding the translation of broad policy guidelines into detailed operational plans. It is hoped that the present review of past experience and of managerial principles may prove of value in either situation.

It is hoped that the study may be of value further to international agencies, interested in the development of a more relevant form of basic schooling for children in Third World countries. Local relevance is in a sense at the opposite pole from conventional aid programmes, which draw upon expertise, curricula and hardware developed in the donor countries. The relevance field has seen its share of misplaced aid – teachers trained to use equipment and materials not available in the schools; imported craft tools kept locked untouched in their polythene packaging, from teachers' lack of confidence in how to use them and from their fear that such scarce resources may be misplaced (and find their way to the black market); Westernised home-science equipment (electric ovens, huge baby's cots and the like) that bears no relationship to the circumstances of the vast majority of pupils' homes. Nevertheless help can be given, particularly as promising ventures often fade away for the lack of finance.

More particularly the following projects may be suggested for international sponsorship.

Project 1. The Development of Low-cost Approaches to Relevance Programmes, Notably to 'Appropriate' or 'Intermediate' Technology Work-experience Programmes (Based on the Use of Local Materials)

This type of research and development work was undertaken in the Kandy centre, Sri Lanka, under Dandeniya's leadership, over the years 1973 and 1974, but the two-year period (with a heavy load of in-service teacher training) was insufficient for the work to come to full fruition. Various Sri Lanka schools made progress in respect of particular resources and technologies. India has long had a tradition of research into simple technologies using local materials, such as soap-making and paper-making, but only the technologies for the ginning, carding and spinning of cotton have found their way extensively into the schools. Interest in appropriate low-cost technologies is now growing in many Third World countries, and their application to schooling could be fruitful notably where balance of payments problems prevent the mass import of school equipment from abroad.

Resource endowments vary between countries and also between the different parts of a single country. Nevertheless, Third World countries do share many resources in common. It would thus be of value for an intensive development programme to be carried out, based in a rural part of an interested Third World country. Publication of the simple technologies devised for school use based on available local resources, and of dissemination techniques, would be of value to educators in many Third World countries. Some work in this direction has been undertaken in the past in connection with science education but the work-experience field has been largely neglected. Experience in Sri Lanka has shown that innovative teachers in the rural areas can build a vigorous pre-vocational studies programme around freely available local materials. Teachers at adjacent schools, however, were at a loss as to how to institute a programme without a large budget. Reference materials in such areas were negligible. Educators in such circumstances, both innovators and those who prefer to follow known paths, would benefit from the availability of documentation in this field (perhaps adapted and translated by national curriculum specialists).

International support for a group of educators in the craft field to work together developing low-cost techniques for resource use and trying them out in selected schools, perhaps as an optional activity, would constitute a major contribution in the work-experience field.

Project 2. Generation of Prototype Teaching Materials for Relevance Topics such as Agriculture and Health, Which Recur in Third World Countries

Project 1. was concerned mainly with the use of local materials for productive purposes. Project 2. concerns the shortage of teaching materials in respect of the various tropical crops, health problems, and so on. The rural teacher may well find difficulty in offering teaching correlated to crops which are important in his own locality, to the life cycle of pests and disease-causing organisms, and so on. A sourcebook relating to such topics would be an invaluable standby for the rural school. In some instances such a sourcebook might be prepared, with international support, on a regional rather than a purely national basis.

Project 3. Support for the Development of a Network of Innovating Relevance-oriented Institutions on the Lines Suggested Under Strategy 1. Above

This would be a broader venture, where a government wished to experiment with the relevance concept on the lines identified here as having exceptional promise. This project would include provision of materials and equipment to participating institutions and the inclusion of ventures such as Projects 1. and 2. above, experiments in teacher-led research and development of resource centres. The suggestions are further highlighted in the section on Strategy 1. earlier in the present chapter.

Project 4. Broadening of the Concept of Educational Planning to Include the Management of Educational Systems and Institutions Generally and of Educational Innovations in Particular

Some effort has been made in the present study to build a bridge between the world of educational management and innovation studies generally and the world of relevance programmes in Third World schools. It has not been possible to undertake a detailed review of the management and innovation literature and its use to the Third World educational planner. As a first step, it would be desirable for an international agency to commission a detailed review of the literature on educational innovation and management, with an evaluation of its utility in the Third World context; and with a survey of existing research in this area relating to Third World countries. This type of material might then be incorporated into the various courses on education planning held under international and national auspices throughout the world. Detailed studies relating to the management of the relevance innovation in particular might further be taken up by agencies with an interest in this field.

BIBLIOGRAPHY

Ahmed, M. and Coombs, P.H. *Education for Rural Development: Case Studies for Planners* (Praeger, New York 1975)

Anderson, J. *The Struggle for the School* (Longmans, Nairobi, 1970)

Batten, T.R. *School and Community in the Tropics* (OUP, Oxford, 1959)

Bernadino, V. *Philippine Community School* (Phoenix Press, Quezon City, Philippines, 1958)

Bizot, J. *Educational Reform in Peru* (UNESCO, Paris, 1975)

Blaug, M. Layard, P.R.G. and Woodhall, M. *The Causes of Graduate Unemployment in India* (Allen Lane, The Penguin Press, London, 1969)

Boakye, J.K.A. *The Continuation School System as a Strategy Towards the Problem of Unemployment Among Middle School Leavers in Ghana: A Preliminary Report* (Centre for Development Studies, University of Cape Coast, Ghana, 1976)

Bolam, R. 'The Management of Educational Change: Towards a Conceptual Framework' in *Management in Education,* Reader 1 (Ward Lock and Open University Press, London, 1975)

Bray, T.M., Dondo, J.M.C. and Moemeka, A.A. 'Education and the Community in Africa: Two Case Studies from Nigeria and Kenya' in King (ed.) (1976), pp.217-38

Callcott, W.H. *Liberalism in Mexico* (Archon Books, Hamden, Connecticut, 1965)

Cameron, J. and Dodd, W.A. *Society, Schools and Progress in Tanzania* (Pergamon Press, Oxford, 1970)

Chin, R., and Benne, K.D. 'General Strategies for Effecting Change in Human Systems' in W.G. Bennis, K.D. Benne and R. Chin (eds.) *The Planning of Change* (Holt, Rinehart and Winston, New York, 1969)

Clignet, R., and Foster, P. *The Fortunate Few: A Study of Secondary Schools and Students in the Ivory Coast* (Northwestern University Press, 1966)

Dalin, P. *Case Studies of Educational Innovation: IV: Strategies for Innovation in Education* (OECD, Centre for Educational Research and Innovation, Paris, 1973)

Davis, R. *Schooling, Work and Reform* (1976, mimeographed)

Dodd, W.A. *Education and Self-reliance in Tanzania: A Study of its Vocational Aspects* (Teachers College Press, Columbia University, New York, 1969)

Dore, R.P. 'Prevocational Studies' in *Marga Journal* (Colombo, 1973), vol. 2, pp.1-17

Figueroa, M., Prieto, A and Gutierrez, R. *The Basic Secondary School in the Country: an Educational Innovation in Cuba* (UNESCO, Paris 1974).

Fischer, L. *Life of Mahatma Gandhi* (Jonathan Cape, London, 1951)

Foster, P.J. *Education and Social Change in Ghana* (Routledge and Kegan Paul, London, 1965a)

Foster, P.J. *The Vocational School Fallacy in Development Planning* (Routledge and Kegan Paul, London, 1965b)

Fresnova, F.P., and Casim, C.P. *Essentials of Philippine Educational System* (Abiva Publishing House, Manila, 1964)

Froebel *The Education of Man* (Appleton & Co., New York, 1887, translator W.N. Hailmann)

Fuggles-Couchman, N. *Report on an Enquiry into Agricultural Education at Primary and Middle Schools* (Government Printer, Dar as Salaam, 1956)

Gandhi, M.K. *An Autobiography or the Story of My Experiments With Truth* (Navajivan Publishing House, Ahmedabad, 1927)

Gore, M.S., Desai I.P. and Chitnis, S. *Field Studies in the Sociology of Education* (National Council of Education Research and Training, New Delhi, 1970)

Government of India, *Quinquennial Review of the Progress of Education in India, 1917-1922*

Graham, C.K. *The History of Education in Ghana* (Frank Cass and Co., London 1971)

Graham, S.F. *Government and Mission Education in Northern Nigeria 1900-1919* (Ibadan University Press, 1966)

Griffiths, V.L. *Teacher-centred: Quality in Sudan Primary Education 1930 to 1970* (Longmans, London, 1975)

Gross, N., Giaquinta J.B. and Bernstein, M. *Implementing Organisational Innovations: A Sociological Analysis of Planned Educational Change* (Harper & Row, New York, 1971)

Hagerstrand, T. 'Quantitative Techniques for Analysis of the Spread of Information and Technology' in C.A. Anderson and M J. Bowman (eds.) *Education and Economic Development* (Aldine Publishing Co., Chicago, 1965)

Harris, A., Lawn, M. and Prescott, W. *Curriculum Innovation* (Croom

Helm, London, and Open University Press, 1975)
Hartog, Sir P. *Some aspects of Indian education past and present* (Oxford University Press, 1939)
Havighurst, R.J. and Neugarten, B.L. *Society and Education* (Allyn and Bacon, Inc., Boston 1962, 2nd edn)
Hawes, H.W.R. *An African Primary Curriculum Survey; Country Profile: Sierra Leone* (University of London Institute of Education Research Report, 1976)
Heafford, M. *Pestalozzi, His Thought and Relevance Today* (Methuen, London, 1967)
Heijnen, J.D. *Development and Education in Mwanza District (Tanzania): A Case Study of Migration and Peasant Farming* (Bronder-Offset, Rotterdam, 1968)
Hingorani, A.T. (ed.) *My Views on Education* (selected writings from M.K. Gandhi, Gandhi Peace Foundation, New Delhi, 1970)
Houghton, H. and Tregear, P. (eds.) *Community Schools in Developing Countries* (UNESCO Institute for Education, Hamburg, 1969)
Hoyle, E. 'Planned Organisational Change in Education' in *Research in education* (1970), vol. 3, pp. 1-22
Jayasuriya, J.E. *Education in Ceylon Before and After Independence 1939-1968* (Associated Educational Publishers, Colombo, 1969)
Jones, T.J. *Education in Africa* (Phelps-Stokes Fund, New York, 1922)
Jones, T.J. *Education in East Africa: A Study of East, Central and South Africa* (Phelps-Stokes Fund, New York, 1925)
Jones, T.J. *Four Essentials of Education* (Scribner, New York, 1926)
Kale, P. *Maharashtra Action Research Project in Occupational Education and Training: Evaluative Research Project in Occupational Education and Training* (Ford Foundation, New Delhi, 1973)
Kazamias, A.M. *Education and the Quest for Modernity in Turkey* (Allen and Unwin, London, 1966)
King, K.J. *Pan-Africanism and Education: A Study of Race Philosophy and Education in the Southern States of America and East Africa* (OUP, Oxford, 1971a)
King, K.J. 'The Politics of Agricultural Education for Africans in Kenya, in *Hadith 3* (East African Publishing House, Nairobi, 1971), pp. 142-56
King, K.J. (ed.) *Education and Community in Africa* (Centre of African Studies, University of Edinburgh, 1976)
Koshy, T.A. 'Research in Basic and Social Education' in *Third Indian Yearbook of Education: educational research* (NCERT, New Delhi, 1968)

Lallez, R. *An Experiment in the Ruralisation of Education: IPAR and the Cameroonian Reform* (UNESCO, Paris, 1974)

Lazerson M. and Grubb, W.N. *American Education and Vocationalism: A Documentary History 1870-1970* (Teachers College Press, Columbia University, New York, 1976)

Lema, A.A. *Education for Self-reliance: A Brief Survey of Self-reliance Activities in Some Tanzanian Schools and Colleges* (Institute of Education, University of Dar es Salaam, undated)

Lema, A.A. *National Attitude and Educational Innovation: A Case Study of Change of Attitude of the Tanzanian Society Towards Education for Self-reliance* (Vienna Institute for Development, 1973)

Lewis, L.J. *Educational Policy and Practice in British Tropical Areas* (Nelson, London, 1954)

Listowel, J. *The Making of Tanganyika* (Chatto and Windus, London, 1965)

Lourié, S. *Production Schools and Rural Employment in Panama* (UNESCO, 1976, mimeographed)

Mbilinyi, M.J. 'The Study of Education and "The Community" ' in King (ed.) (1976), pp. 81-96

Meera, C. *National Survey of Elementary Teacher Education in India* (National Council of Educational Research and Training, New Delhi, 1970)

Miles, M.N. 'Innovations in Education' (Teachers' College Press, New York, 1964)

Morris-Hale, W. *British Administration in Tanganyika from 1920 to 1945* (University of Geneva, 1969)

Morrison, D.R. *Education and Politics in Africa: The Tanzanian Case* (Hurst and Co., London 1976)

Mort, P. 'Studies in Educational Innovation from the Institute of Administrative Research: an Overview' in Miles (ed.) (1964), pp. 317-28

Moshi, E.E. 'Community Education Centre: The Tanzanian Experience' in King (ed.) (1976), pp. 116-17

Mwobahe, B.L. and Mbilinyi M.J. (eds.) *Challenge of Education for Self-reliance* (Institute of Education, Dar es Salaam, 1975)

Myers, C.N. *Education and National Development in Mexico* (Princeton University, New Jersey, 1965)

Naik, C. *Educational Innovation in India* (UNESCO, Paris, 1974)

Naik, J.P. 'Elementary Teachers in India – A historical survey' in *Indian Year Book of Education, 1964 – Elementary Education* (National

Council of Educational Research and Training, New Delhi, 1964)
Narain, I. 'Rural Local Politics and Primary School Management' in S.H. Rudolph and L.I. Rudolph (eds.), *Education and Politics in India: Studies in Organisation, Society and Policy* (Harvard University Press, Mass., 1972)
Nimpuno, K. 'Design for Community Education: General Propositions and Case Study Material on Community Education Centres in Tanzania' in King (ed.) (1976), pp. 189-216
Noorani, A.G. *President Zakir Husain: A quest for Excellence* (Popular Prakashan, Bombay, 1967)
Nurullah, S. and Naik, J.P. *A History of Education in India (During the British Period)* (Macmillan, Bombay, 1951)
Nyerere, J.K. *Education for Self-reliance* (Government Printer, Dar es Salaam, 1967)
Olsen, E.G. *The School and Community Reader: Education in Perspective* (Macmillan, New York, 1963)
Orata, P.T. 'Community Schools in the Philippines' in *Prospects in Education* (UNESCO, Paris, 1969), vol. 1, no. 1
Orata, P.T. *Self-help Barrio High Schools: The Story of 250,000 Students Earning Their Education and Preparing Themselves for Life* (Eastern Universities Press and SEAMEO Regional Centre for Educational Innovation and Technology, Singapore, 1972)
Peabody, F.G. *Education for Life: The Story of Hampton Institute* (Doubleday, New York, 1918)
Peters, R.S. *Authority, Responsibility and Education* (Allen & Unwin, London, 1959)
Peters, R.S. *Ethics and Education* (Allen & Unwin, London, 1966)
Ponsioen, J.A. (ed.) *Educational Innovations in Africa; Policies and Administration* (Institute of Social Studies, The Hague, 1972)
Psacharopoulos, G. (assisted by K. Hinchliffe) *Returns to Education: An International Comparison* (Elsevier Publishing Co., Amsterdam, 1973)
van Rensburg, P. *Report from Swaneng Hill* (Dag Hammarskold Foundation, and Almquist and Wiksell, Stockholm, 1974)
Rogers, E.M. and colleagues *Diffusion of Innovations: Educational Change in Thai Government Secondary Schools* (Institute for International Studies in Education, Michigan State University, East Lansing, Michigan, 1969)
Rogers, E.M. and Shoemaker, F.F. *Communication of Innovations: A Cross-cultural Approach* (Free Press, New Yrok, 1971)
Rudd, W.G.A. 'Teachers as Curriculum Developers: A Second Generation

Viewpoint' in Taylor and Walton (eds.), *The Curriculum: Research, Innovation and Change* (Ward Lock, London, 1973), pp. 38-9 and 52-64

Ruiz, R.E. *Mexico: The Challenge of Poverty and Illiteracy* (Huntingdon Library, San Marino, California, 1963)

Salamatullah *Thoughts on Basic Education* (Asia Publishing House, London, 1963)

Salamatullah 'Basic Education: Retrospect and Prospect' in *Indian Year Book of Education, 1964 – Elementary Education* (National Council of Educational Research and Training, New Delhi, 1964)

Semin, R. 'Education in Turkey' in *Year Book of Education* J.A. Lauwerys and N. Hans (ed.) (Evans Brothers, London, 1952)

Sinclair, M.E. 'Education and the Community: A First Look at the History of Attempts to Introduce Productive Work into the Primary School Curriculum' in King (ed.) (1976), pp. 45-80

Sinclair, M.E. *Gandhian Basic Education (Notes, Comments*, no. 12, Unit for Cooperation with UNICEF, UNESCO, Paris, 1976)

Smith, F. *A History of English Elementary Education, 1760-1902* (University of London Press, 1931)

Solaiman, M. *The Comilla Rural Education Experiment* (Bangladesh Academy for Rural Development, Comilla, Bangladesh, 1975)

Solarin, T. 'The Mayflower School in Nigeria' in Ponsioen (ed.) (1972), pp. 121-8

Sommer, J., Kale, P. and Gupta, R. *Rural Development at the Grassroots – The Catalyst Role* (Ford Foundation, New Delhi, 1974)

Spencer, S.R. *Booker T. Washington and the Negro's Place in American Life* (Little, Brown & Co., Boston, 1955)

Stenhouse, L. *An Introduction to Curriculum Research and Development* (Heinemann, London, 1975)

Stewart, W.A.C. and McCann, W. *The Educational Innovators* (Macmillan, London, 1967/8)

Stone, F.A. 'Rural Revitalisation and the Village Institute in Turkey: Sponsors and Critics' (Comparative Education Review, 18, 1974)

Tannenbaum, F. *Ten Keys to Latin America* (Vintage Books, New York, 1966)

Thuraisingham, V. 'A New Orientation – Work Experience' in *Education in Ceylon: Centenary Volume* (Ministry of Education and Cultural Affairs, Colombo, 1969)

Tompkins, P. and Bird, C. *The Secret Life of Plants* (Penguin Books, New York, 1974)

UNESCO *Six Community Schools of the Philippines* (National Commission of the Philippines, Manila, 1955)

UNESCO *Qualitative Aspects of Educational Planning* (International Institute of Educational Planning, Paris, 1969)

UNESCO *Curriculum Development for Work-oriented Education* (*UNESCO* Regional Office for Education in Asia, Bangkok, 1975)

Vexliard, A. and Aytach K. 'The Village Institutes in Turkey' in *Comparative Education Review* (8, 1964)

Weeks, S.G. *Community School in Africa: Is There a Lesson for Papua, New Guinea?* (University of Papua, New Guinea, Education Research Unit Report No. 15)

Wilson, J. *Education and Changing West African Culture* (Teachers College, Columbia University, New York, 1963)

INDEX

The letter-by-letter system has been adopted